This book is dedicated to the memory
of my parents

*Alexander and Adele
Yudin*

Who with their sterling character and integrity
laid a foundation for future generations of proud
observant Jews.

I was privileged to be their son.

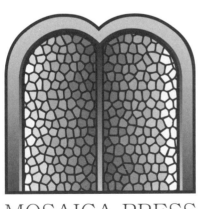

MOSAICA PRESS

RABBI BENJAMIN YUDIN

on the Parsha

Mosaica Press, Inc.

© 2013 by Mosaica Press

Edited by Doron Kornbluth

Typeset and designed by Rayzel Broyde

All rights reserved

ISBN-10: 1937887162   ISBN-13:978-1-937887-16-2

Published and distributed by:

Mosaica Press, Inc.

www.mosaicapress.com

info@mosaicapress.com

In memory of

Alfred Szylit

ARI BEN SHMUEL

אֲרִי בֶּן שְׁמוּאֵל

His brave mother placed him on the Kindertransport days after his Bar Mitzvah.

While his entire family perished in the Shoah, he was privileged to see his grandchildren become Bar and Bas Mitzvah.

In honor of

OF CAMP MONROE

A true friend and inspiration who encouraged and enabled
me to embark on this project.

CONTENTS

7

Contents

Contents

"TOMORROW, WE HAVE THE PRIVILEGE"
was the immediate, instinctive way I
began my first radio program over
three decades ago.

ACKNOWLEDGMENTS

There are no words to adequately express my deep-felt and overwhelming *hakaras ha-tov* to Hashem for the ability to bring this volume to fruition. As I write this, in the week of *Parshas Bo*, I am reminded of the *Meshech Chachmah* who explains that in the *tefillin shel yad*, the four *parshios* are in one parchment in one compartment, as it symbolizes the love Hashem has for all Jews, which is the same. The *tefillin shel rosh* contain the same four parshios in four separate compartments, as it represents the *hashgacha pratis* / Divine Providence that He extends, and in this area, each individual receives a different share. I am truly humbled by the *hashgacha pratis* that He has afforded me throughout my life. In retrospect, I can appreciate the different influences, and these in turn have opened me not only to love and appreciate all Jews, but to accept and incorporate Torah from many different sources.

My parents, *a"h*, sent me to Crown Heights Yeshiva, where I was privileged to meet and study under Rav Aharon Kreiser, *zt"l*. He not only influenced me to attend Rabbi Jacob Joseph High School, but later on he honored me by serving as a clearing house, either

13

approving or sharply rejecting the particular idea for my weekly radio broadcast. His helping me to focus and his critical analysis is a lesson that remains with me. I attended Camp Gan Yisrael of Chabad for several summers, which influenced me in a positive way towards *kiruv*, sensitivity for the soul, and *Chassidish* writings. Attending Yeshiva University and learning from my *Rabbeim*, including Rav Dovid Lifshitz, *zt"l* and Rav Soloveichik, *zt"l* opened my mind for the excitement and sweetness of Torah. I am especially grateful for the opportunity to teach at the J.S.S./Mechina school of Yeshiva University, catering to young men constantly questioning, and providing them with a foundation for growth. Teaching them caused me to wrestle with the fundamentals of our religion, which has been especially helpful in my broadcasts and teaching. The *dibuk chaverim*, the ability to be nourished by outstanding *Rabbeim* and colleagues at Yeshiva, including Rav Hershel Schachter, *shlita*, and Rav Mordechai Willig, *shlita*, whose constant *halachic* guidance and sage counsel have been most valuable to me over the years. I am indebted to Rav Baruch Simon, *shlita*, who has introduced me to many different sources and ideas, all of which have contributed to the varied tapestry of these *divrei Torah*.

I am blessed with an outstanding *shachein tov*, Rav Eliyahu Chaim Swerdloff, *shlita*, the *Rosh Yeshiva* of Yeshiva Gedola of Paterson, who shares of his incredible wealth of Torah with me, and whose insights are always helpful and appreciated.

My weekly broadcasts have facilitated two long distance *chavrusas*. For many years I have enjoyed the close camaraderie and benefited greatly from the insights of Rabbi Yaakov Weiner, Dean of the Jerusalem Center for Research. His additions have contributed greatly to this work. Further *hashgacha pratis*; about five years ago I *davened* one morning in Herziliya, and immediately enjoyed the manner in which Rabbi Akiva Rottenberg presented the *Daf haYomi*. We have been learning together almost weekly ever since.

I am privileged and blessed with a wonderful Congregation, Shomrei Torah in Fair Lawn, New Jersey, where I began my rabbinical career over four decades ago, and I can say with pride that the honeymoon is still on. My daily interaction with the Congregation, the shiurim and sharing real life events, has been both humbling and especially enriching. I thank them for sharing me with my listening audience, and now for the opportunity and assistance in writing this book.

I am truly appreciative of the many loyal listeners of WFMU: JM in the AM for challenging me on a weekly basis to identify an aspect of the parsha that will hopefully be meaningful, educational and inspirational for the knowledgeable and the not-yet knowledgeable members of the listening audience. The preparation time invested into these programs is often many hours, but the privilege accrued therefrom is both immediate and long lasting.

I thank Nachum Segal for the outstanding programming with which he has provided listeners over the years, for creating the respect and environment for both Rabbi Goldwasser's and my *divrei Torah*, and for facilitating and enabling me to disseminate Torah.

I was impressed with Aliza Weinstein's writing talents when she lived in Fairlawn prior to going on aliyah. The shiurim she gave to the women were always clear, concise and appreciated. Her transcribing ability is demonstrated by not only transmitting the information, but including the tone and flavor as well.

Rav Yaacov Haber is a yedid nefesh with whom I have been sharing *divrei Torah* with for many years. His insight and creativity always impresses me. I am honored that he and Mosaica Press agreed to publish this work, and appreciate all his talented expertise that helped shape the actualization of this work. Rabbi Doron Kornbluth has the gift of *Rashi*, to transmit and convey much material and information in a concise manner. I am most appreciative of his transforming these broadcasts and making them reader-friendly. I pray that Rabbis Haber and Kornbluth be blessed with good health and the ability *l'hagdil Torah u-l'ha'adirah*.

It has been especially sweet to have gained and shared insights on the *divrei Torah* with all of our children. Their input and interest in "the broadcast" serves to connect the entire immediate family.

Special thanks to Rabbi Andi Yudin, who took it upon himself to review the entire manuscript.

Rebbe Akiva attributed his accomplishments in Torah to his wife Rochel. I have been so blessed with my dear wife Shevi, who excels in those self-same traits Rebbe Akiva attributed to Rochel. Shevi's understanding, devotion, sacrifice and love are legendary. Above and beyond, she has freed me of many responsibilities in the home, allowing me to learn and teach. The many Thursday nights and, of late, Wednesday nights devoted to these broadcasts are a tribute to her partnership in my *mitzvah* of *Talmud Torah* and *harbatzas Torah*. May Hashem repay her for her selfless devotion to me, to our children and to the entire Shomrei Torah community.

INTRODUCTION

"Tomorrow, we have the privilege" was the immediate, instinctive way I began my first radio program over three decades ago. Over these past many years, I have never tired of repeating this introduction and I have only grown in amazement at the term and application of the word 'privilege'.

The dictionary defines privilege as a right or benefit that is given to some people and not to others. I understand this on both a communal and personal level. *Torah tzivah lanu Moshe* — the Torah, the teaching that Moshe commanded us, is the heritage of the assembly [nation] of Yaakov. A heritage, in contrast to an inheritance, is to be safeguarded and perpetuated. The nation of Israel has been charged to study and disseminate Hashem's Torah. This is accomplished through the written word, and we live in an age that sees the incredible proliferation of the written form of Torah. Books in all languages in all areas on Jewish life: Talmud, halachah and philosophy are constantly emerging. In addition, the radio is used to broadcast Torah and religious inspiration. Radio station WFMU has been meeting the challenge, and exercising this privilege for over thirty years.

On a personal note, I realize how privileged I am to share insights and lessons from Torah with many, familiarizing them with a theme of the weekly *parsha*, and showing its relevance and pertinence to our age.

Norman Laster, a member of the Fair Lawn Jewish community began hosting a daily radio program from the campus of Upsala College in New Jersey. He invited me to share a Torah thought on *Parshas Bo*, and I agreed, not realizing this would be the beginning of more than thirty years of weekly radio broadcasts.

Understandably, the biggest challenge that I faced, and still do, was finding the happy medium between the different segments of the broad listening audience. Nachum Segal on his popular JM in the AM program reaches Lakewood, Monsey and Boro Park, as well as Franklin Lakes, Pompton Lakes and other communities where the level of knowledge and practice is vastly different. I never cease to be inspired myself by the ability of Torah to bridge and connect the entire spectrum of the broad Jewish community. Moreover, with the internet today, Torah connects Jews in different continents.

Emes yesh lo raglayim — literally, the truth has feet — is an expression used by our Rabbis to denote that something truthful and meaningful can stand by itself, be understood, appreciated and admired by all. Thus, our Torah which is eternal, has the capacity to speak to each and every generation, and teach basic values that can inspire and uplift.

I am a firm believer that the Shabbos meals are not only an opportunity for families to join together, creating familial bonds that span lifetimes, but they are an opportunity to show the importance and centrality of Torah by sharing and injecting thoughts on the weekly *parsha*, thereby providing nourishment not only for the body but for the soul as well. I often find myself referring to a particular insight or commentary as delicious. Ideally, as the food not only nourishes but provides a literal *oneg* — pleasantness and enjoyment, so too the *divrei Torah* and *zemiros* should uplift and elevate the meal to that of a religious experience. I know that many have used the various broadcasts to enhance their Shabbos table, and for this I am grateful and humbled to know that in some small measure I have contributed to the spirituality of their Shabbos table.

The enclosed *divrei Torah* were each initially presented as an approximate fifteen minute *dvar Torah* on the radio. They have been edited to enable the reader to actually bring a book to the table and provide a Torah thought and opportunity for further discussion.

Finding a thought that could be appreciated by most listeners has always been my biggest challenge. I have used as my litmus test throughout that which excites me; I attempt to share that excitement that evokes from a particular interpretation and commentary.

It is my fervent hope and prayer that these Torah thoughts that emerged from my heart will enter the hearts of the readers and in some small way impact on their *Weltanschauung*.

BEREISHIS
TOWARDS A JUST WORLD

The *sefer Som Derech* by the late Rav Simcha Zissel Brody, *zt"l* of Chevron Yeshiva in Yerushalayim, has a fascinating approach to the beginning of the Torah. Thet *gemara* in *Avodah Zarah*[1] quotes Rav Chiya bar Abba in the name of Rabbi Yochanan who says that *Sefer Bereishis* is called *Sefer Hayashar* (the Book of the Just) because Avraham, Yitzchak and Yaakov were called *"yesharim,"* proper and just in their behavior. Bilaam, of all people, referred to the *Avos* as *"yesharim"* upon claiming *"tamos nafshi mos yesharim"*[2] — May I be privileged to die as the Patriarchs died. Rav Chiya bar Abba refers to this verse to show that *Sefer Hayashar* refers to *Sefer Bereishis*, the majority of which is an account of the lives of the Patriarchs.

In addition, perhaps there is another reason that *Bereishis* can be referred to as *Sefer Hayashar*: From the first chapter of *Bereishis* we can see that God infused into nature itself the concept of *yashrus*, that man should conduct himself in a manner which is just, righteous and proper. We will see three examples of this idea.

---

1   25a.
2   *Bamidbar* 23:10.

The Justice of the Land of Israel

We begin with the very first comment of Rashi on the Torah. On the verse, *"Bereishis bara Elokim,"*[3] Rashi quotes Rabbi Yitzchok, who states that the Torah really should have begun with the verse, *"Ha-chodesh ha-zeh lachem,"*[4] the first commandment which the Jewish people received as a nation. Why then does the Torah begin with *Sefer Bereishis*? *Lehavdil eleph havdalos*, the personal anecdotes of George Washington and Thomas Jefferson and their families are not included in the American Constitution! Why does the Torah, our constitution, *lehavdil eleph havdalos*, include so many anecdotes? Rabbi Yitzchok gives an incredible answer. *Mishum "koach ma'asav heegid le'amo"*[5] *laseis lahem nachalas goyim*, namely to teach the Jewish people God's power in order to give them the justification for receiving the Land of Israel. The nations of the world may say to the Jewish people, as indeed history has proven until this day, *"listim atem,"* you are robbers, because you conquered the land which the seven nations had inhabited. Our answer is, *"Bereishis bara Elokim"* — the whole earth belongs to God. He created it and He gave it to whomever He wanted. Initially, it was His wish to give it to the seven nations. And then by His will, He took it from them and gave it to us. Think about it, though: if we were to give this answer to most non-Jews, would they be satisfied?

In truth, Rashi is talking to each and every Jew: we must realize that our claim to the Land of Israel is completely justified — and totally just. When we conquered the Land, both in the days of Joshua and in 1948, it was 100 percent legitimate, honorable and correct — in compliance with that which God told us. Furthermore, in case any doubts arise as to the justice of our case, God began the Torah with *"Bereishis bara Elokim."* The name used is *Elokim*, indicating *midas ha-din*, justice. The world is based upon justice, adding credence to our legitimate and just claim to the Land of Israel.

---

3   *Bereishis* 1:1.
4   *Shemos* 12:2.
5   *Tehillim* 111:6.

The Justice of the Night Sky

Second, on the fourth day of creation we are told that God made the two great luminaries, the great light to illuminate the day and the smaller, lesser light to rule the evening.[6] Rashi quotes the *gemara* in *Chulin* 60b, which relates that the two luminaries were originally created equal in size. The moon complained to God that it is impossible for two kings to share one crown. God agreed with the moon and made it smaller. However, to counterbalance this punishment and appease the moon, He created quadrillions of stars to add light to the night sky. Even though God justifiably diminished its size, He went the extra mile to appease the moon!

How much are we to learn from this one act of *lifnim mishuras ha-din* of Hakadosh Baruch Hu — if we hurt someone, even justifiably, we are to go out of our way to appease them, help them and encourage them.

The Justice of Consultation

Finally, the Torah tells us, *"Na'aseh adam"*[7] — Let us make man. *Gevalt!* Us? How many gods are there?! Of course, there is only one God. Such a provocative statement may leave room for *apikorsim*, those who are skeptics, to suggest that there might be more than one god. The Torah, however, tells us (in the plural) that Hashem consulted with His *pamalya shel maalah*, His Heavenly Court, in order to teach that the *gadol*, the one who is at the top, should *notel reshus min ha-katan*, show respect and take permission from the lesser one. To do so is to act with humility, *derech eretz* and justice.

How do we apply these lessons to our daily lives? Even though you may be the CEO of a corporation, sincerely ask your staff for their thoughts. It gives people a feeling of importance, and it is the *right* way to act.

---

6   *Bereishis* 1:16.
7   Ibid., 1:26.

It is this that the Torah is teaching us when it includes and, all the more so, begins with the account of creation. It is not simply an account of what happened on day 1, day 2, etc., which we do not understand anyway because as Rashi teaches everything was actually created on the first day. Rather, it is best expressed by what we say from *Tehillim* every Shabbos and *Yom Tov*, "*Ha-shamayim misaprim kevod kel*" (*Tehillim* 19:2), the Heavens speak the glory of God. What is this beautiful glory of God? It is this incredible sensitivity that God built into nature.

As we start the new *Bereishis*, a new studying of the Torah, we should try to incorporate this sensitivity into our lives and thereby heed the message of *Sefer Hayashar* by acting in a proper, just, and righteous manner.

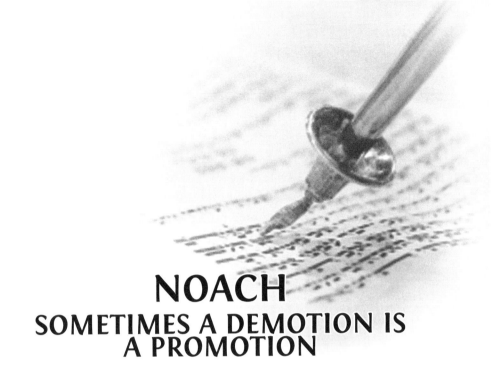

NOACH
SOMETIMES A DEMOTION IS A PROMOTION

Immediately after the flood recedes and Noach leaves the Ark, the Torah tells us, *"Va-yiven Noach mizbei'ach la'Hashem,"*[8] he builds an altar for Hashem and brings offerings on the altar.

The verse then says, *"Va-yomer Hashem el leebo,"* the Torah gives us the opportunity to listen in as God speaks to Himself, *ka-viyachol*. What does He say? *"Lo osif le'kalel od es ha-adamah ba'avur ha'adam,"* I will never again continue to curse the ground because of man. Additionally, *"ve'lo osif od le'hakos es kol chai ka'asher asisi,"* nor will I ever again, literally, blot out every living being as I have just done.[9]

What has changed? On the one hand, if mankind deserves to be destroyed then why not destroy them again? On the other hand, if mankind did not deserve to be destroyed then why did Hashem bring a flood in the first place?

The *Be'er Yosef*, Rav Yosef Salant, brings a very interesting in-

---

8   Ibid., 8:20.

9   Ibid.

sight into the transformation which occurs prior to and following the flood.

When God created man, He blessed him not only "*v'kivshuha,*" he is to conquer (to subdue the natural resources of this world) but also "*u'ridu,*" he is to have control over all of nature.[10] This control (or dominion) over nature can be positive or negative. Sadly, it didn't turn out well. As man became corrupt, so too, the world became corrupted. As the Rabbis tell us at the end of *Parshas Bereishis*, God decided to kill the animals as well. Why? They were mating not with their own kind. They learned from man! Also, approximately three *tefachim* (about a foot) of the land itself[11] had to be washed away and uprooted. Why? The earth itself was influenced by human corruption such that if one seed was planted, a different kind would grow. This unnatural situation had to be eradicated, and indeed Hashem brought a *mabul* (flood).

After the flood however, points out the *Be'er Yosef*, man is no longer granted "*u'ridu.*" He is no longer given this dominion over nature. Hashem says, "*U'morachem ve'chitchem yeeyeh al kol chayas ha-aretz,*"[12] meaning that the fear of you and the dread of you shall be upon every beast of the earth. There should be awe and fear of man, but man is no longer given this dominion over nature.

A great transformation has occurred. Before the flood, man has external domination over all of nature. After the flood, Hashem says, I am no longer going to curse the *adamah* because of man "*ki yetzer lev ha'adam ra mi'neurav,*"[13] because man's heart is evil from his youth — there is an internal struggle for good and bad within man. Post-flood, man is told that he has to focus on internal domination.

What can he accomplish? The verse says,[14] "*Va'yarach Hashem es rei'ach ha-nichoach,*" Hashem smelled the pleasing aroma. This is itself inherently problematic. Given that God is incorporeal, what

---

10   Ibid., 1:28.

11   Except in *Eretz Yisrael.*

12   Ibid., 9:2.

13   Ibid., 8:21.

14   Ibid.

does it mean that He smelled the pleasing aroma of the offerings?! First, however, permit me to precede it with the idea of the *Ma'aseh Hashem*, a *Rishon* who is disturbed about an aroma. He says that unlike the senses of touch, sight and hearing, there is something different about the sense of smell. Imagine the following scene: You are fidgeting with your keys at the front door to your house. You have not yet entered your house, and already you can smell precisely what is for dinner. You have not seen it nor have you touched it, and yet there is an awareness and an anticipation before there is any actual contact.

The *midrash* explains that "*Hei'rei'ach reicho shel Avraham Avinu*," God smelled the scent and the pleasant aroma of "*Avraham oleh mi'kivshan ha-esh*," Avraham miraculously surviving the furnace into which he was thrown. Hashem smelled that furnace. "*Va'yarach*" — what does that mean? Hashem literally smelled the *rei'ach* of Chananiah, Mishael and Azaryah, the three young *tzaddikim, oleh mi'kivshan ha-esh*. They too were thrown into the furnace, later on in Jewish history by Nevuchadnezzar, and miraculously were saved. The idea is that God saw their incredible *mesiras nefesh*, their incredible devotion. He saw the incredible dominion that man is capable of asserting over himself, the kind of individual He can make. Hashem was amazed at the extent of the potential of man. He consequently says, I will no longer eradicate man and all of society.

On the one hand, there has been a diminution. There is no longer this *u'ridu*. On the other hand, however, there is this tremendous potential about which the *parsha* is reminding us that man has the capacity to attain and achieve.

What do we find in the following *parsha*? Regarding Avraham Avinu, the Torah tells us "*ve'he'emin ba'Hashem*," that he believed in God. "*Va-yachsheveha lo tzedakah*,"[15] Rashi interprets the second part of this verse to mean that Hashem looked upon this faith as an act of righteousness, of *tzedakah*. Not only does the Torah teach us that God showers man with goodness, but the greatness of man is that he

---

15   Ibid., 15:6.

can reciprocate and give *tzedakah* to Hashem. He can give his righteousness, which can bring *nachas* to his Father in Heaven. Just as a loving father cares for his children and provides for them, so too does mankind as His devoted children have the capacity to bring *nachas ruach*, to bring satisfaction and pleasure to God.

Rav Yisrael Salanter said, "When I came into this world I thought I would be able to have an influence over the entire world. As I grew older, I narrowed my expectations such that I would be able to have an influence over my country. As I matured, I narrowed them further to my city. Afterwards, I restricted them to my family. After that, I restricted them further to my children. Finally, I had narrowed my expectations of influence all the way down to myself."

That is the transformation which occurred at the time of the flood. On the one hand, man has been reduced. He no longer has the same dominion over nature which he once had. That is why, in a good way, God will never destroy the entire world again. On the other hand, God is always ready, willing and able to smell our goodness — to see how the great potential that we have will, please God, be activated in the future.

LECH LECHA
IT'S IN OUR BLOOD

The first chapters of *Bereishis*, as we know, deal with the creation of the world and mankind. *Parshas Lech Lecha* deals with creation of a different kind, that of *Am Yisrael*, the Jewish people. The term for creation in Hebrew is *bara*. Rashi explains the meaning of this word as, *yesh me'ayin*, literally something from nothing. Just as the world came into being literally out of nothing, similarly *Parshas Lech Lecha* describes the creation of the Jewish people as a form of *yesh me'ayin*.

In the beginning of chapter 2 of *Bereishis*, we are taught, "*Eleh toldos ha-shamayim ve'ha-aretz be'hibaram*" (v. 4). This is the genealogy, the unfolding, of heaven and earth when they were created. The *Baal HaTurim* on this verse tells us that the (Hebrew) letters of *be'hibaram*, when switched around, actually spell *be'Avraham*. The idea is that God created the world for Avraham and the Jewish people. What does this mean? It means that even historians, and even someone like Mark Twain, were able to recognize and realize that there is something very unique about the Jewish people. Despite the fact that the world has ever been attempting to persecute and annihilate us, we are still here. We say it every year at the Pesach Seder. *"B'chol dor va'dor omdim aleinu le'chaloseinu,"* in every generation, one way or another, they try to annihilate the Jewish people. *Ve'HaKadosh Baruch Hu matzileinu mi'yadam,"* and Hashem delivers us from their hands.

The unique status of the Jewish people is portrayed so powerfully by Rabbi Yehuda Halevi, in his *Sefer Kuzari.* He postulates that there are four strata of matter in this world. First, there is the *domem*, the inanimate object. After which comes the *tzomei'ach*, that which grows. Then there is the *chai*, the animals, and *midaber*, man. Above these four levels, says Rabbi Yehuda Halevi, is *Yisrael*, the Jewish nation. This has to bespeak to the Jewish people the incredible responsibility which we have. Our mission and purpose is to follow the lead of Avraham Avinu, our forefather Avraham.

What is the uniqueness of Avraham such that he has become the model for us? The opening verse of our *parsha* states, *"Va-yomer Hashem el Avram, lech lecha me'artzecha u'mi'moladetecha u'mi'beis avicha el ha-aretz asher arekha."*[16] God speaks to Avraham and says to him, you are to leave your land, your birthplace, your father's home, and go to the Land which I will show you.

This appears to be the first time that God speaks to Avraham. Later, the Torah relates that Avraham entered Eretz Canaan and passed through the land. Afterwards, we are told, *"Va'yera Hashem el Avram,"* Hashem appeared to Avraham.[17] First God spoke to him, and only later appeared to him.

The *Or Hachaim Hakadosh* asks a very insightful question. Generally, when God communicates with someone, first He appears to them and then He tells them what it is that He wants from them. For example, by the burning bush in *Parshas Shemos*, the Torah tells us that God appears to Moshe from the bush itself. *"Va'yera"*[18] — God appears to Moshe, and then He proceeds to speak to him. Why is there a change here in what would appear to be the logical order? It

16   *Bereishis* 12:1.
17   Ibid., 12:5-6.
18   *Shemos* 3:2.

makes sense that God would first appear to Avraham and later communicate with him; why did God change the order?

The *Or Hachaim Hakadosh* gives a very interesting answer. Following Avraham, every individual to whom God appears has a sense of belief and trust in God. From where did they get it? From none other than Avraham Avinu himself. Just as a father literally passes down his DNA to his children, so too Avraham Avinu passed down belief in God. It went to Yitzchak and Yaakov and all the way to Amram and Moshe. Amazingly, it is also true for us as well. It is literally in our blood. Because they had an innate sense of belief in God, He could appear to them. Without true belief, God cannot appear to a person.

Avraham, however, did not have anyone who would pass belief down to him. He did not inherit innate belief in God; quite the opposite, as his father was an idol worshipper! Hashem couldn't simply appear to Avraham just yet: *She'lo hera shechinaso eilav ad she'bachan oso im mikayem gezeirosav*, He does not appear to Avraham until He tests him to see if he would be willing to follow His decrees.

What is a decree? A decree is like a *chok*, a law which defies reason. Why, after all, does Avraham have to leave his home? Further, why does he have to leave an elderly father? Why can't he teach monotheism in his homeland?

The answer is that Avraham is being asked to do something which is *le'maalah min ha-teva*, something which is against his nature. Only by doing so could he truly exhibit his true belief in God, and allow God to appear to him.

We know that Avraham Avinu passed ten tests. According to the Rambam, the first test was that of *Lech Lecha*. Would Avraham leave his birthplace and his father and travel endlessly, not knowing where he was going, all for God's sake? The answer is that he does, of course, leave, and thereby successfully passes the test. Rashi respectfully disagrees with the Rambam. He claims that there was an earlier test than that of *Lech Lecha*: being thrown into a furnace in order to prove his belief in God.

Why does the Rambam not count this as a test? Perhaps we can say the following: Throughout world history, there have been individuals who have been intensely committed to a cause, whatever the name of that cause may be. For example, at the time of the American Revolution, the infamous cry of "Give me liberty or give me death!" could be heard. For a person to give his life for a cause is, in and of itself, not so fantastic. It is not so unusual because, in reality, the person believes in something so strongly to the extent that he would be willing to give his life for it. However, the greatness of Avraham and the test of *Lech Lecha* was something which Avraham could not understand. Even though he could not understand it, nevertheless this is what made it a test. He was able to go against his nature.

This is such a powerful idea and there is a very profound lesson in it for all of us. We fulfill so many *mitzvos*, especially man to man, that we can understand. For example, when we hear that someone is sick we go to visit them at the hospital. If someone unfortunately loses a relative and they are sitting *shivah*, we go to comfort them. These are all Biblical *mitzvos*. However, these are all *mitzvos* which we can understand. These are *mitzvos sichlios*.

Avraham distinguished himself by doing that which he could *not* understand. He acted solely because God told him to do so.

Avraham was tested to see if he would comply with that which Hashem told him to do, whether he understood it or not. We, the proud progeny of Avraham, walk in his path. He "proved" himself through his willingness to follow God even when he didn't understand the Almighty's commands. We too should be proud to follow the laws of Hashem, whether we understand them or not.

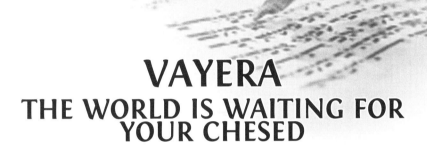

VAYERA
THE WORLD IS WAITING FOR YOUR CHESED

The *parsha* begins with an incredible contrast. Avraham Avinu had every excuse in the book *not* to do kindness. It was three days after his surgery of *bris mila*, circumcision. Avraham, however, is more pained by the fact that he cannot extend hospitality to guests than even the pain of his circumcision. Therefore, because of Avraham's incredible desire to help others, God affords him the opportunity to do so and sends guests.

Compare this with the story which immediately follows (there is not even a break between the *parshios*). The Torah describes the nature of *Sdom* and *Amora*, the antithesis of the generosity and the benevolence of Avraham. Not only do they refrain from *chesed*; even worse, they don't let other people do *chesed*!

A rather significant lesson emerges from the opening of *Parshas Vayera*. It can be encapsulated within three words found in *Tehillim*,[19] where David HaMelech says *"Olam chesed yibaneh,"* that our world is literally based upon kindness, meaning it is not just "another mitzvah."

19   89:3.

In truth, there are *mitzvos* and there are *mitzvos*. The late Reb Yehuda Leib Kagan, *zt"l*, in his *sefer Halichos Yehuda*, notes that within *mitzvos* there are gradations. There are *mitzvos* of a *yachid*, meaning that an individual performs a mitzvah by and for himself such as putting on *tefillin*, shaking the *lulav*, etc. There are also *mitzvos* of the *rabim*, that which a person does which affects many. Certainly, the latter is of a higher nature than the former.

Chesed, kindness, is such a mitzvah of *rabim*. Look at how much each one of us affects and has an effect on one another. The *gemara* in *Brachos*[20] teaches us that Ben Zoma once saw a very large multitude of Jews and said, "*Baruch she'bara kol eilu le'shamsheini*." Note, he said, how God created all these people to serve *me*, because we serve one another.

The *gemara* continues to speak about that which Ben Zoma was wont to exclaim. "How many exertions the first man had to do in order to "have his cake and eat it too." He had to plow, sow, reap and gather the stalks. Then, he had to thresh them, winnow the chaff from the grain and select the other waste from the grain. Next, he would grind the grain into flour, sift the flour, knead it into dough and bake the dough. Finally and only after all these steps, he was able to eat the resulting bread. "As for me," says Ben Zoma, "I get up in the morning and it is all there waiting for me at the *makolet* (grocery store)."

Ben Zoma was likewise inclined to marvel at all the exertions which the first man had to do in order to be able to put on a garment. He had to shear the wool, clean it, disentangle it, spin it into thread, weave the thread, and then and only after all these steps he was able to make it into a garment. "As for me," says Ben Zoma, "I can just go down the block and purchase a garment."

What emerges is the idea that each and every one of us enables the rest of society to function. Each of us is essential. We think that we are simply going to work in the morning in order to make a living. This is true. However, we must realize and appreciate the privilege

---

20   58a.

and opportunity to do kindness that each and every one of us has. If you are in a profession and vocation in which you help people, such as a doctor, a nurse, a teacher or a rabbi, where you are directly involved with people, or if you are in sales and are providing goods which people need — there are so many opportunities that you have to help another. Therefore, before and as you enter your place of business, think to yourself that you are doing so not only to make a living, but also to enhance the world which God has put us in.

In the introduction to the *sefer Nefesh Hachaim*, the son of Reb Chaim Volozhiner, Reb Yitzchak, writes about his father's incredible acts of kindness. He explains that even when his father was old and could not do much for other people any longer, he nevertheless did what he could and prayed on their behalf. He writes as follows, "My father would rebuke me because he noticed that I was not as empathetic and sympathetic to the needs of others. This is what he would say to me constantly, 'This is the essence of man. Man was not created and born only and primarily for himself, but rather to help, to affect, and to influence others as each person has his or her potential to do.'"

In the words of Rav Kagan, *zt"l*, society, which is one big cooperative, should realize how much— with proper cooperation— we help and enhance one another. What a privilege it is to participate in the ongoing nature of this world, *olam chesed yibaneh,* in which each and every one of us, through our kindnesses, improves and makes this world a much better place.

CHAYEI SARAH
MINCHAH – AN EXCHANGE OF GIFTS

R abbi Yosi b'Rabbi Chanina in *gemara Brachos*[21] teaches us that *tefillos avos tiknum*, the prayers we have were instituted by the Patriarchs. Avraham returns *"el ha-makom asher amad sham es pnei Hashem,"*[22] to the place where he was standing before Hashem. The Talmud proves that this verse means that he was praying. The Torah also says (in several places[23]) *"va'yashkem Avraham baboker,"* Avraham rose early in the morning, thereby showing that Avraham instituted the morning prayer.

In our *parsha*, the Torah tells us that when Eliezer is bringing Rivka back to the house of Avraham, Yitzchak goes out to the field. *"Va'yetze Yitzchak lasuach basadeh lifnos arev,"*[24] Yitzchak went out to supplicate in the field towards evening. The Talmud learns from here that Yitzchak is responsible for instituting the afternoon, or *Minchah,* prayer.

---

21   26b.
22   *Bereishis* 19:27.
23   Ibid.; 21:14, 22:3.
24   Ibid., 24:63.

Finally, from a verse in *Parshas Vayetzei*, the Talmud learns that Yaakov Avinu is the one who instituted the *Maariv* service.

So, as hinted to in our *parsha*, Yitzchak institutes the *Minchah* prayer. No small thing: the *gemara* in *Brachos*[25] teaches us a very interesting lesson. The Talmud quotes Rav Chalbo as saying in the name of Rav Huna, "*Hizharu, l'olam yehei adam zahir b'tefillas haMinchah,*" be especially careful regarding the prayer of *Minchah*, "*she'harei Eliyahu lo ne'eneh ela b'tefillas haMinchah,*" for behold Eliyahu benefited specifically from the *Minchah* prayer. This is the well-known story in the first Book of Kings,[26] when Eliyahu Hanavi challenges the hundreds of false prophets to a clear confrontation once and for all to see if their *Baal* is God or in fact *Hashem hu HaElokim*, Hashem is God. Each of them, both Eliyahu and the hundreds of false prophets, take an animal and build an altar. They put wood, but do not apply the fire. Eliyahu says to them, "You call on the name of your gods and I will call on the name of Hashem, and the God that answers by fire He is God."[27] They try, and Eliyahu makes fun of their lack of success. We are then told in the *Navi*, "*Vayehi ba'alos haMinchah,*" it was at the time of *Minchah* that Eliyahu steps forward and prays "*Aneni Hashem aneni,*" God, please respond.[28] The rest is history. The fire comes down from Heaven and consumes Eliyahu's offering.

Why did Eliyahu specifically wait until the time of *Minchah* to pray to Hashem?

The Rashba explains that these false prophets believed that the sun had independent power and that Hashem did not control the world. Therefore, Eliyahu waited until the end of the day when the sun was setting. He was thereby demonstrating that precisely at the time when their god was waning, the fire would descend, and Hashem would manifest His absolute control. They believed that their gods had powers, but the truth is that whatever power it may have had waned, and even then the true God's power never waned. Our

---

25   6b.

26   Ch. 18.

27   Kings I 18:24.

28   Ibid., 18:36-37.

daily recitation of this prayer echoes Eliyahu's demonstration that Hashem controls nature — always.

The Aruch Hashulchan, in his introduction to the prayer of *Minchah*[29], tells us that *Minchah* is particularly favorable because it corresponds to the last offering which was brought every day. Moreover, it is as beloved as the *Neilah* service on Yom Kippur. Just as *Neilah* closes the Yom Kippur service, so too the *Minchah* offering closed the service in the Beis Hamikdash every single day. Furthermore, *Shacharis* is recited before a person becomes preoccupied with all the pressures and details of earning a living. *Maariv* is said in the evening when one has distanced himself from the concerns of the work day. *Minchah*, however, is recited (especially during the shorter days of the winter months) when one is still at work. This is often a great challenge and sacrifice as it is a two-fold process. First, it requires that one extricate him or herself, not only physically but mentally. Second, he or she must then focus on the special relationship of the Jew with God and the responsibilities which accompany that relationship.

Indeed, it is most appropriate that Yitzchak is the one who instituted *Minchah*. As we know, Avraham personifies the *middah* of *chesed*, kindness. Yitzchak represents *gevurah*, strength. It takes an additional strength of character and commitment to interrupt one's day and pray. Yitzchak possessed this strength of character, which he infused into not only this prayer but into this time zone. He thereby laid the path for us to draw on his strength in order to extricate ourselves from that which we are doing and to partake in the prayer of *Minchah*.

Interestingly, Rav Shimson Raphael Hirsch, in his commentary on the Torah, notes that the very three prayers which the Patriarchs instituted reflect their respective lives. Avraham lived a life of *Shacharis*. Even though he faced challenges, he was nevertheless accepted by the entire society as *nesi Elokim*.[30] He was prosperous and he was given the child that he wanted. There was a lot of positivity and sunshine in his life. Yitzchak, however, lived a life of *Minchah*.

---

29   *Orach Chaim* 232:1-2.
30   *Bereishis* 23:6.

Minchah can only be recited at a time when the sun is waning, on its way down. Yitzchak lived this time. He was not as accepted as his father. In fact, unfortunately, he was bothered by the locals. In addition, the 400 years that God says to Avraham that his children will be strangers in a land not theirs commences with the birth of Yitzchak. While Yitzchak never left the Land of Israel, he was a stranger in his own land. Hence, one can say that Yitzchak represents and reflects the very prayer that is to be recited only when the sun is setting. Yaakov lived a life of nighttime. He experienced the hatred of a brother, the difficulties of a father-in-law, the great challenge of sons pitted one against the other. Yaakov lived a life of night, of darkness. His prayer is therefore that of *Maariv*.

In our own lives, perhaps we can explain why *Minchah* is so important. Because *Minchah* is recited precisely at the time when the Jew is in the marketplace, when he is in the field hard at work. Therefore, exactly at such a time when one is involved in his worldly activities one is to realize and recognize that it all comes from God. While he is out there in the office, he might be led to believe that he is having a good day today because of *kochi ve'otzem yadi*[31] — it must be my talents, my ingenuity and my creativity which has given me all my success. No! The *Minchah* prayer helps the Jew to focus. It gives him the understanding that all his possessions, talents, ideas — all of his success only comes through Hashem.

This leads to a fascinating philosophical insight. Why do we even have to pray in the first place? If God is going to give something to me, He can give it to me irrespective of my prayer. The answer is that maybe the only reason that you are given your success is *because* you connect yourself to God! It is our very recognition of our dependence on God and our connection to Him that makes a person worthy of His blessings!

May our review of the prayer of *Minchah*, alluded to in *Parshas Chayei Sarah*, encourage us to attend or create a *Minchah minyan* at work, and thus enable us to truly connect to God, and enjoy His blessings.

---

31   *Devarim* 8:17.

TOLDOS
LABOR PAINS AND THE BIRTH OF TORAH

The Torah tells us that Rivka experienced unusual pain during the early part of her pregnancy. What does she do? *"Va'teilech lidrosh es Hashem,"*[32] she goes to seek the word of God in order to understand the unusual distress which she is undergoing.

The prophet tells her, *"Va'yomer Hashem lah, shnei goyim be'vitneich u'shnei leumim me-mayayich yipareidu,"* you are carrying two nations, and these two regimes shall literally separate from inside of you. What will be the nature of their existence? *"U'le'om mil'om ye'ematz,"* literally, the might shall pass from one to the other. In other words, there is going to be a struggle between the two of them. Which one will have the upper hand? Will it be the elder, Esav, whom we know historically as Rome, or will it be the younger, Yaakov, Israel? *"Ve'rav ya'avod tza'ir"*[33]; ultimately, Rivka is promised that the elder shall serve the younger.

---

32   *Bereishis* 25:21-22.
33   Ibid., 25:23.

The *parsha* does not just begin with this struggle. At the very end of the *parsha* too, after Yitzchak has already blessed Yaakov, Esav comes and begs his father for another blessing for himself. Yitzchak responds: *"Ve'haya ka'asher tarid u'farakta ulo me'al tzavarecha."*[34] It will be that when your brother shall literally be down, when he will fail to keep his Torah and *mitzvos*, at that time you will be able to literally cast off his yoke from your neck. Then, you will gain superiority over him. The struggle between the two nations is characterized as a "see-saw effect" — when one is pulled down, the other rises up. The struggle in her womb is the struggle of history: Rome vs. Jerusalem.

Consider the very interesting concept of *kri* and *kesiv*. The Torah oftentimes will write a word one way and have it pronounced another way. There is such an occurrence in our *parsha*. When the prophet tells Rivka that she has "*shnei **goyim** be'vitneich*", the word is pronounced *goyim*, meaning two nations. It is written in the Torah, however, with two *yuds*. It could very well be read (and is understood by our Rabbis in *Avodah Zarah* and *Brachos)*, to mean *shnei gaiyim*, literally meaning two proud ones. Which two individuals are being referred to?

The Talmud teaches that these individuals are none other than Rebbi and Antoninus. They lived approximately around the second and the third century C.E. Rebbi was the head of the Jewish community and Antoninus was the head of the Roman people. Interestingly, they were good friends. Our question is: Why, in the middle of a prophecy, speaking of the enmity and tension which is going to exist between the two brothers, Yaakov and Esav, does the Torah choose to teach us about the close friendship of these two leaders?

Let us learn a little about them. The Tosfos in *Avodah Zarah*[35] tells us of amazing *hashgachah pratis* regarding the birth of Rebbi and Antoninus. The *gemara* in *Kiddushin*[36] tells us that on the day that Rabbi Akiva died, Rebbi was born. We know that the time of

---

34   27:40.
35   10b.
36   *Kidushim* (72b).

Rabbi Akiva's death was one of great persecution. At that time, there was a decree against circumcision. Rebbi's father circumcised him nonetheless. The local governor learned of this, and ordered him and his wife to bring their circumcised baby before the Caesar — which meant certain death. As they were traveling to the Caesar, the mother of Antoninus had compassion on Rebbi's mother, and switched her baby, Antoninus, with Rebbi. This kindly Roman matron took little Yehuda, later to become Rebbi, and Rebbi's mother took the uncircumcised Antoninus before the Caesar, avoiding all punishment.

Tosfos goes one step beyond. Rebbi's mother even nursed Antoninus! This certainly contributed to the close friendship between Rebbi and Antoninus later on in their lives. According to one opinion, as quoted in the *Yerushalmi*, says Tosfos, perhaps it even explains how Antoninus actually studied Torah and literally converted and circumcised himself when he grew up.

With this background, we can better understand what the prophet responded to Rivka. The Ramban explains that the prophet was telling Rivka not to be afraid. The agitation, the pain, and the suffering are all brought on because she is currently pregnant with twins. This is the way of twins, especially when the children will found two nations, which will hate one another. Therefore, the prophet assures her that the tension between the children is temporary, and from now on, things will be calm within her womb.

Rav Simcha Zissel Brody, *zt"l*, the Rosh Yeshiva of the Chevron Yeshiva, in his *sefer Som Derech* asks why the prophet emphasizes that calm will eventually prevail. He answers that even though there will be tension and difficulty for the Jewish people throughout the millennium, there will nevertheless be a time when Rebbi and Antoninus will be the best of friends. This friendship will enable Rabbi Yehuda Hanasi (Rabbi Judah the Prince), Rebbi, to author, redact and edit the *Mishnah*, which is the foundation of the Oral Law. The Talmud is built upon the Oral Law. If the Torah, which we are still studying today, has survived, it is because of Rebbi. The Torah was in danger of being lost and Rebbi, based on the verse in *Tehillim*,[37] "*Eis la'asos laHashem heifeiru torasecha*," it is a time to act for God, put the Oral Law literally into print in order that it should survive. It has certainly survived! His emergency measure of creating the *Mishnah* was so important in Jewish history that it has its own recognition within the prophecy to Rivka! (The Torah, instead of writing *goyim*, two nations, writes *gaiyim*, thereby making reference to two great men, as that is an integral part of the prophecy). What we see therefore from *Parshas Toldos* is this incredible *hashgachah pratis*, Divine Providence, over the survival of Torah.

The bottom line which emerges from our *parsha* is the incredible *hashgachah pratis*, Divine Providence, which has maintained Torah throughout the years. We have seen it in our own day as well. For example, during the Holocaust, there was the escape of *Yeshivas Mir*, which was wrought with all kinds of Divine intervention going completely against the odds. The yeshiva went through Siberia to Shanghai, and then to America. The journey of the yeshiva served as the fulfillment of that which Reb Chaim Volozhiner, *zt"l* said about how the Torah would go into ten *goluyos* before returning to Eretz Yisrael. America, he said, would be one of those great stations of Torah. It was the Mir Yeshiva which helped establish America as one of these great stations of Torah. We see this before our eyes — the great emergence of Torah study throughout the world, in Eretz Yisrael as well as in America.

The *parsha* reminds us about God's incredible *hashgachah* to protect Torah throughout history. . Each of us should also stop and reflect on the *hashgachah pratis* in our lives, whether it be with our families, or our *parnassah*. This is an incredible time for us to literally give great thanksgiving to Hakadosh Baruch Hu for all the *hashgachah pratis* that He affords us — in *gashmius* and *ruchnius*.

---

37   119:126.

VAYETZEI
THE FIRST STEP

The *parsha* opens by describing Yaakov's dream of a ladder with its base on the ground and its head towards the heavens; Angels of God are ascending and descending it.[38]

The *Midrash Tanchuma* explains which angels Yaakov saw. Each nation has its own ministering angel "up above." In this dream, God showed Yaakov the angels of each of the four nations which were destined to rule over the Jewish people in the future. First, He shows him the angels of the nation of Bavel, ascending and descending. Then, He shows him the angels of Madai, ascending and descending. Yaakov then sees the angels of Yavan as well as those of Edom, ascending and descending respectively.

Afterwards, God turns to Yaakov and tells him to ascend the ladder as well. Yaakov, however, is afraid — perhaps, just as the angels go up and then come down, so too if he went up he would eventually be forced down as well. God assures Yaakov that if he goes up the ladder, he will not fall. What an incredible *midrash*!

We know the concept of *ma'aseh avos siman la'banim*. The

---

38   *Bereishis* 28:12.

narratives which the Torah provides us are not simply historical accounts. The narratives reveal the unfolding of Jewish history. We are to see ourselves in these stories. When we sit in *shul* on *Shabbos Parshas Vayetze* and listen as the Torah describes the ladder and the angels ascending in Yaakov's dream, we are to hear the *ba'al koreh* calling to each and every one of us: We, who bear the name "Yaakov," are to ascend. Each and every one of us has to aspire towards growth. We should not be satisfied where we are.

It is interesting that God implanted a natural drive within each and every individual to better himself. Each person strives to be the best that he or she can be, whether the goal is to get more money, fame, prestige, etc. These are healthy drives, which Hashem puts in us in order that we should be successful. Just as we have this drive in the area of livelihood, of parenting, and in all areas of life, commensurately we must have this drive in our *avodas ha-kodesh* — the manner in which we relate to God, the Jewish people and Jewish causes.

Life has a *tachlis,* a purpose. Therefore, a true and authentic corollary of this *emunah*, this belief, is to be as productive as possible. God put us in this world to do a job. He put us in this world in order that we serve Him. We should not be satisfied with a minimal type of service where a person endeavors to only comply with the letter of the law. Rather, we want to truly be able to feel the dictum which we recite twice a day in the *Shema*, "*Ve'ahavta es Hashem Elokecha*,"[39] you are to love God, and therefore do as much for Him as we can. Our performance of the *mitzvos* should not remain static. We should always try to have a deeper and greater appreciation of them. Do we strive to have that special, beautiful pair of *tefillin* similar to the upgrades we have on our cars and on our appliances? Is our Shabbos *kiddush* the same as that which we recited ten and even twenty years ago, or do we have a deeper and greater appreciation thereof? How can we improve the kindnesses which we do? Just as we work to improve our business' bottom line, similarly, in the realm of the spiritual, we must aspire to continually "go up the ladder" and to do more.

---

39   *Devarim* 6:5.

The *midrash*[40] gives three examples as to why some people do not get on the ladder. The first example given describes a rather large mound of earth. The foolish person says, "My goodness! How can I ever move this mound?" while the wise man says, "I will take two shovels today and two shovels tomorrow."

Similarly, the *midrash* continues, the foolish person says, "Who can study the Torah? *Nezikin* contains therein *Bava Kama*, *Bava Metzia*, *Bava Basra*, each consisting of ten chapters combining for a total of thirty chapters. *Keilim* has thirty chapters in and of itself. The Torah is so vast. It is beyond me." However, the wise man says, "Two *halachos* today, two *halachos* tomorrow, and eventually I will be able to study as much of the Torah as I can."

The second analogy which the *midrash* uses portrays a loaf of bread, symbolic of our sustenance, suspended high on the ceiling of the kitchen. The foolish person looks up and says, "My goodness! Who can bring it down? I cannot reach it." However, the wise man says, "I will get a pole and I will attach even another one to it. Then, I will be able to get it down because, after all, did not somebody else put it there in the first place?"

Similarly, the fool says, "How can I study Torah, which, after all, is in the domain of the elite and the wise?" On the other hand, the wise man says, "Did he not have a teacher? I too can have a teacher, and therefore I will learn as well, two *halachos* today and two tomorrow."

The third analogy is that of an individual who hires workers to clean and wash strainers and sieves. The fool says, "My goodness! What will I accomplish with this?" The wise man says, "If this is what he wants and he will pay me for it, then this is what I shall do."

Similarly, the fool says, "Why should I study Torah? What good is it? I am going to forget it. The many holes, I cannot retain it all." The wise man, however, finds value in just the study itself. God commanded it, so it is surely of inestimable value. It purifies, enhances, enriches and makes the individual a better person.

There are many different excuses why a person is afraid to take

---

40   *Vayikra Rabbah* 19:2.

that first step and to get on the ladder. God said to Yaakov, "Yaakov, if you get up there, I assure you that you will not fall." There is a very special *hashgachah pratis* in spiritual endeavors: If a person takes that first step, He assures us that there will be further success up that ladder.

Let me share a kind of initiation I gave my own children when they were each approximately three to four years old. I stood them on a staircase, which had about five to six steps. I put them first on the first or second step, held out my arms, and said to them, "Jump." They were not so far off the ground, and after a moment they jumped into their father's arms. A minute later, I put them on the next step. They looked somewhat concerned as if to say, "Can I do it?" Their father put his arms out and said, "Jump and I will catch you," and they jumped. Then I put them on the next step up. Sure enough, they hesitated, but they jumped this time as well. I believe they learned a very important lesson from this exercise. Somebody loves them, is there to guide them, to catch them when they find themselves in trouble, and to allow them to grow.

Parshas Vayetze calls out to each and every one of us: "Don't be afraid to take that first step!" Set up a *chavrusa*; if you incorporate Torah study as part of your weekly routine, your week will be enhanced and enriched. Focus on improving your prayer, or do more acts of *chesed*. Whatever you do, take the first step, and, please God, the many *brachos* which God promised Yaakov will be fulfilled with each and every one who ascends the ladder.

VAYISHLACH
AN EDUCATED JEW IS GOD'S BEST CUSTOMER

Parshas Vayishlach is a *parsha* of confrontation. The *parsha* opens with the following scene. An extremely nervous and anxious Yaakov is preparing for a meeting with his brother, Esav. This would be the first time in twenty years they would meet after Yaakov had run away from his brother when Esav threatened to kill Yaakov.

Rav Elchonon Wasserman, *hy"d,* in his *Kovetz Maamarim*, has a fascinating insight on our *parsha*. However, in order to properly appreciate his ideas, it is necessary to shed light into what contributed to his greatness. Rav Wasserman was born in 1875 and died in 1941. He studied under the great Rav Shimon Shkop, *zt"l* and later under Rav Chaim Brisker, *zt"l*. At the age of thirty-two, he joined the *Kodshim Kollel* of the Chofetz Chaim, who subsequently became his lifetime role model. In 1921, he became head of the yeshiva in Baranovitch where he remained for the rest of his life. When the Chofetz Chaim planned to make *aliyah*, a delegation of Rabbis came to plead with him to stay in Europe. As the spiritual leader of Eastern European Jewry, he was sorely needed, and they protested his decision to abandon them. The Chofetz Chaim eased their concerns by assuring them that he would leave Rav Elchonon behind. This is just a little bit of the greatness of Rav Elchonon Wasserman.

Let us now proceed to share the Torah of Rav Elchonon.

In our *parsha*, we are taught *"Va'yivaser Yaakov levado, va'yayavek ish imo ad alos ha-shachar,"*[41] Yaakov was left alone, and a man wrestled with him until the break of dawn. The *midrash* in *Bereishis Rabbah*[42] identifies the attacker as the guardian angel of Esav, and the Tanchuma adds that his name is Sama'el.

Rav Elchonon asks a fascinating question: Why is it that this angel, whose mission is to protect Esav and his culture, waited until Yaakov to attack? Why did he not wrestle with Avraham and Yitzchak?

Rav Elchonon gives a most profound answer. He cites the *Yerushalmi Chagiga*, whereby we are taught that Hashem is patient and can overlook even the three gravest sins of idolatry, adultery and murder. Which sin, however, does Hashem not forgive? He does not forgive the sin of *bitul Torah*, neglect of Torah study. Rav Wasserman explains that when two adversaries fight one another, even if one side is victorious today the other side can regroup and come back with a vengeance tomorrow. However, if the first side seizes the weapons and ammunition of the other, leaving the second side totally defenseless, the war is over, forever.

The *gemara*[43] teaches when Hashem created the *yetzer hara*, the evil inclination, He simultaneously created the antidote to control and defeat it — the study of Torah. The angel Sama'el, representing the *yetzer hara*, knows that the only force which can overpower him is Torah. Therefore, when the Jewish people, God forbid, are deficient in their study of Torah, they have, in effect, surrendered their armaments and weapons, and are powerless to fight back.

It is for this reason, Rav Wasserman argues, that Avraham and

41 *Bereishis* 32:25.
42 77:3.
43 *Kiddushin* 30b.

Yitzchak were not attacked by Sama'el. Avraham represents the pillar of *chesed*, bequeathing kindness and benevolence to his progeny. Yitzchak is the pillar of *avodah*, prayer. It is Yaakov, however, who resides in the tents of Torah, and is thus the target and the victim of the *yetzer hara*. Rav Wasserman quotes his Rebbe, the Chofetz Chaim, who said that the *yetzer hara* does not mind if the Jew does kindness, fasts, and prays all day long — as long as these activities are to the exclusion of Torah study.

In the introduction to *Mesilas Yesharim*, Rav Moshe Chaim Luzzatto quotes the Kabbalist Rabbi Hershel Ostropola, *zt"l* who recounts the following experience: Prior to the Chmielnicki massacres, the Satan came to him in a dream and told him that he was prepared to rescind the decrees against the Jewish communities of Central Europe. There was only one condition: They had to stop learning Torah. Rabbi Ostropola refused the Satan's offer. Clearly, he understood the importance of Torah study.

In *Parshas Vayishlach*, we read *"Va'tayka kaf yerech Yaakov,"*[44] Yaakov's hip socket was dislocated during the wrestling match with the guardian angel of Esav. The commentaries understand the symbolism of this encounter in the following way: When the angel sees that he cannot topple Yaakov, he strikes a serious blow to Yaakov's descendants. They are deflected from *talmud Torah* by either persecution or assimilation. Additionally, the *Zohar* likens *"yerech Yaakov"* to *tomchin d'oraisa*, the supporters of Torah. Rav Wasserman writes that the people prior to the coming of the *Mashiach* will not realize the importance of *talmud Torah*. Many Jews will support other Jewish causes, but Jewish education will not be a priority.

However, we must ask *why* the Torah is the antidote to the *yetzer hara*. First, the more one studies Torah, the more one's level of observance is enhanced. Moreover, Torah, and the study of Torah alone, has the ability to transform one's character and personality. When one studies Torah, which is *kudsha brich hu ve'oraisa chad hu*, God and his Torah being inseparable, he literally imbibes Godliness.

---

44   *Bereishis* 32:25.

How exactly does Torah have such an incredible effect upon the personality? The *gemara* in *Chulin*[45] relates the encounter of Pinchas ben Yair at the river Ginai. When R' Pinchas ben Yair arrived at Ginai, he ordered the waters of the river to split and they followed suit. The *Ohr Hachaim Hakadosh* suggests and states the following. Pinchas ben Yair lives after Sinai. He is coming with Torah under his belt. Torah permeates his very being. It is therefore not such a wonder that he, with Torah, is able to cause the sea to split.

Let us conclude with a heart-breaking, eyewitness report of the execution of Rav Elchonon Wasserman and his students, *hy"d*, on the eleventh of Tammuz 1941. Rav Elchonon was taken with his students from amidst their studying Torah to their place of execution. Rav Wasserman said, "It seems that in heaven they consider us righteous people as we have been chosen to atone with our bodies for the Jewish people. We must therefore repent immediately. The time is short. We must keep in mind that with our repentance our sacrifice will be more pure and with that we will save the lives of our brothers and sisters in America. The fire that will consume our bodies, that very same fire, will rebuild the Jewish people."

How important and powerful is the study of Torah? The answer is, very.

---

45   *Chulin* (7a).

VAYESHEV
SMALL ACTIONS WITH BIG IMPACT

Parshas Vayeshev is one of those *parshios* which does not get easier from year to year. It represents the first step of the implementation of that which God told Avraham in no uncertain terms back in *Parshas Lech Lecha*. In *Bereishis* chapter 15, verse 13, the Torah relates God telling Avraham, *"Yado'a tayda ki ger yi'hiyeh zaracha b'eretz lo lahem va'avadum ve'inu osam,"* you shall surely know that your children will be strangers in a land which is not theirs and they are going to be enslaved as well as persecuted."

How does this unfold? It unfolds through the act of selling Yosef down to Egypt, which occurs in *Parshas Vayeshev*.

The Torah tells us, *"Va'yishma Reuven va'yatzilayhu miyadam,"*[46] Reuven heard and saved (Yosef) by suggesting that the brothers throw Yosef in a pit rather than kill him. The Torah tells us that Reuven's ultimate intent was to return Yosef back to his father.

What is it that Reuven exactly heard?

---

46   37:21.

According to the *chachamim* in the *midrash*,[47] he heard Yosef's dreams. *Parshas Vayeshev* begins with Yosef telling his brothers of his two dreams.[48] The first dream depicted the brothers out in the field and their bundles bowing down to Yosef. The second dream depicted the scene of eleven stars bowing down to Yosef. Reuven hears Yosef telling these two dreams, and views them through a semi-prophetic lens. He says, "Yosef counts me among my brethren despite the act which I had done inappropriately."

Which act so concerned Reuven? After Rachel died, Yaakov's bed was in the tent of Bilha, Rachel's maidservant. Reuven, out of affection and devotion to his mother, moved his father's bed to his mother Leah's tent. This was certainly an inappropriate act on Reuven's behalf, and he did *teshuvah*. Still, he was afraid that as a result he would lose his stature from among the tribes. Then, he hears Yosef referring to eleven stars, including him! He therefore says, "Look what my brother has done for me and I will not save him in return?!"

Did Yosef have the intent of being kind to Reuven? The answer is, absolutely not. Reuven, nevertheless, did derive benefit therefrom. Therefore, Reuven is teaching us a very important lesson. If one receives benefit from someone else, even if only inadvertently, one has to be appreciative and express thanksgiving to that person.

Similarly, in *Parshas Vayetze*, the Torah relates that Rachel finally has a child. What does she name him? "*Va'tomer asaf Elokim es cherpasi vatikra es shmo Yosef,*"[49] she calls him Yosef because God "has gathered in my disgrace." On the surface this means that until now she had no children. However, Rashi cites an incredible *midrash*, which says the following: As long as a woman does not have a child, she has no one to blame for all the little things which go wrong in the house. Once she has a child, she can blame them on the child. For example, her husband comes home and asks, "Who broke this?" She can now say, "Your son broke it." He says, "Who ate the brownies?" She can say, "Your son."

47   *Bereishis Rabbah* 84:15.

48   *Breishis* 37:7-9.

49   30:23-24.

Of all the names by which to call Yosef! There are many more appropriate names. For example, we find later in the *parsha*, when Yosef is in the house of Potifar, the Torah describes Yosef as an *"ish matzliach,"*[50] a most successful man. What a nice name "Matzliach" would have been! Rav Zilberstein gives another suggestion concerning possible names for Yosef. When Yaakov blesses Yosef, he says *"ben poras Yosef."*[51] Call him "Poras," Rav Zilberstein proposes[52], as it means graceful. Instead, what does Rachel call him? She calls him "Yosef." Why? Although she knows that this son will bring her incredible *nachas* in a large way, nevertheless, she is ever appreciative of the small things in life.

This is a very important lesson which emerges from these *midrashim*. The Torah is not only teaching us to be thankful and grateful for the big things in life, but to appreciate the smaller things as well. Consider the famous *midrash* about Yisro's daughters, who were regularly bullied by the male sheperds. When Yisro asks his daughters, "How is it that you are home so early today?"[53] they respond: *"Ish mitzri hitzilanu mi'yad ha'ro'im,"* an Egyptian man saved us from the other male shepherds. On the surface, the Egyptian man is none other than Moshe. However, the Rabbis identify this Egyptian man as the one whom Moshe killed, as a result of which Moshe had to flee Egypt. In consequence of his running away, Moshe was able to save Yisro's daughters. The *midrash* compares this situation to a person who is bitten by an animal. His foot is all swollen and ablaze with heat. He runs to the well in order to immerse his foot in the waters and when he gets there, he sees that just a moment or two before a child has fallen into the well. He consequently saves the child. When the family of the child thanks him, he says, "Don't thank me. Thank the insect that bit me. That is what ultimately saved your child."

We could go through life in one of two ways. We can either have an attitude whereby we take everything for granted, or we can be

---

50   *Bereishis* 39:2.

51   Ibid., 49:22.

52   *Aleinu L'Shabeach Breishis* pg. 389

53   *Shemos* 2:18-19.

grateful for everything we have. The *gemara* in *Brachos*[54] relates a teaching by Ben Zoma: What does a good guest say? "Look at all the trouble (i.e., cooking and cleaning) which the host has undergone for me." He could have said, "He [the host] had to do all these things anyway for his own family. He did not do it specifically for me." Ben Zoma teaches that the proper attitude is to be appreciative of even the small things in life.

The late R' Yechezkel Sarna, zt"l, explains that every time one *bentsches* he thanks God for giving him the food *"b'chen b'chesed u'verachamim."* What does it mean that God sustains us and nourishes us *b'chen*, with grace? God could have nourished us in black and white. The foods did not have to come in all the different colors in which they are currently found. When you think about it, the fact that your salad is so multi-colored makes the eating experience that much more enjoyable. The little things in life are that which we are to be most appreciative of.

As *Parshas Vayeshev* is usually read around the time of Chanukah, it is appropriate to note that this lesson can be learned from Chanukah as well.

On the holiday of Chanukah we are to let the candles burn *ad she'tichle regel min ha-shuk*,[55] literally meaning until people stop walking in the street. The Sfas Emes explains that this refers to *regilus*, habituation. Most people are always ready to say Thank you for the big things in life. Comes along Chanukah and reminds us that we should be grateful *"al ha-nisim,"* not just the big ones but for the everyday miracles which God constantly performs on our behalf — and be grateful for the help we have received from others, whether they intended it or not!

---

54   58a.
55   *Shabbos* 21b.

MIKETZ
THE TRUTH HURTS

One of the most dramatic scenes in history is the confrontation between Yosef and his brothers. We must ask a basic question: How is it that the brothers do not realize that they are standing before Yosef? In order to fully understand the question, we must realize that the brothers listened to Yaakov when he told them[56] not to attract attention while they are in Egypt. How are they to go about this feat? They each enter Egypt via a different entrance. Meanwhile, Yosef enacted a law, whereby each and every individual who came to purchase food had to sign in their name and their father's name. Somehow, the brothers did not find this strange. The names are brought to Yosef every night, and Yosef is thus able to see for example, that Reuven ben Yaakov is here, Shimon ben Yaakov is here, etc.

Yosef sends out his men to collect these individuals and bring them to him. Among the thousands of people (as the Torah tells us, *"Ve'chol ha'aretz ba'u Mitzraima,"*[57] entire lands came to purchase

---

56   *Bereishis Rabbah* 91.
57   *Bereishis* 41:57.

from Egypt), somebody took the trouble to round up the brothers. While the charge of espionage of which they are accused is a serious one, it does not generally warrant being brought immediately to the viceroy for interrogation! And yet, that is exactly what happened to them. Why then do they not find their ordeal quite strange?

In addition, when they are standing before Yosef or, as they believe him to be, Tzofnas Panei'ach, he takes out his cup and he says as follows: "Based upon this *neechush*, divination, I could tell that two of you killed out a city. I could tell that you sold your brother." Rashi[58] tells us that Yosef even told them the nature and color of their respective beds in the Land of Canaan. My goodness, how could an Egyptian viceroy possibly know this?! He tells them that he is getting this information through divination. They know that there is no substance to idolatry or divination. And yet, they go along with this story because after all, Tzofnas Panei'ach is talking to them.

Furthermore, how is it that when they bow down to Yosef they do not immediately stop in their tracks and say to themselves, "Wait a second, this is somewhat reminiscent of a dream"? These dreams obviously disturbed them enough to the extent that they sold their brother!

When the brothers come down to Yosef a second time, what happens?

The Torah tells us that Yosef has his servants prepare the meal for them "*U'tvoach tevach ve'hachein.*"[59] The *gemara*[60] explains that Yosef made sure they knew that the *gid ha-nasheh* was removed from the animal so that it would be glatt kosher for them to eat. Again, they have no clue that they are in front of Yosef.

Finally, Yosef puts placecards by the table. He does not ask them who is oldest and thus who is second, third, etc. He nevertheless puts them all in their right places. This move at least evokes some

---

58   Ibid., 43:7.
59   Ibid., 43:16.
60   *Chulin* 91.

kind of response from them. The Torah relates that *"va'yismihu,"*[61] the brothers looked at each other with astonishment.

Yet, still, they don't recognize their brother. They knew he was sold down to Egypt. Shouldn't it have been obvious by now? How do we explain the fact that the brothers could not and would not acknowledge that they were in front of Yosef?

Rav Nevenzahl, the Rav of the Old City, suggests a very powerful answer. The brothers could have easily admitted that it was indeed Yosef who was behind all the strange occurrences which befell them in Egypt. However, that would thereby be acknowledging that all the grief and suffering which they had caused their father for twenty-two years, all the grief and suffering they had caused Yosef, all that they had caused their grandfather, Yitzchak, all this was for naught. To recognize Yosef would be to admit that his dreams were right, that he was a *tzaddik*, and that what they had done was very, very wrong. Therefore, rather than admit the obvious, that they were wrong, they deceived themselves to believe that they were standing before Tzofnas Panei'ach.

This is a very important lesson, which may be applied especially at Chanukah time (generally when *Parshas Miketz* is read). The Ramban writes, at the end of *Parshas Bo*, that the reason that God brings *nisim gluyim*, open miracles, is to help us understand that *nisim nistarim*, the everyday actions which go on about us, are not simply natural but they are all directed from God. The problem is that we do not easily admit it. The brothers of Yosef refused to recognize the obvious until Yosef actually hit them over the head with the truth and openly revealed himself. Similarly, we do not realize that just as God causes the oil to last for eight days, so too He directs and governs our daily lives.

The Talmud tells us that Chanukah was established for the purpose *"lehodos u'lehallel"* (*Shabbos* 21b). There are two understandings of the word *"lehodos."* The verb *lehodos* means, first and foremost, to admit. First we must admit that it comes from God. Then, once we

61   *Bereishis* 43:33.

acknowledge that it all comes from God we can truly give thanks to Him.

Each and every one of us, starting today and continuing each and every day, should try and find another reason for admitting, acknowledging and thanking God for what He does for us daily. For example, Thank you Hashem for my good health. Thank you Hashem today for giving me my house, family and job. We have so much that we fail to actually recognize that it *all* comes from God. Perhaps we are afraid that doing so will cause us to have to change and improve our lifestyle.

Chanukah comes but once a year. Let us take advantage of this amazing God-given opportunity and learn this very important lesson — it all comes from God.

VAYIGASH
CHESED TO THE UNDESERVING

Parshas Vayigash is an especially emotionally charged *parsha*. Being separated from his brothers for twenty-two years, Yosef finally reconnects with them. Moreover, Yosef had also been separated from his father for at least the same length of time. Yehuda, in this *parsha*, describes the relationship between Yaakov and Yosef as *"venafsho keshura venafsho,"*[62] literally, their souls are bound up one with the other. They too are reunited in *Parshas Vayigash*.

When he reveals his identity to his brothers, Yosef notices their bewildered demeanors and says to them, *"Ve'atah al tayatzvu ve'al yichar be'eineichem ki mechartem osi hayna,"* and now don't worry or feel guilty that you have sold me here. Rather, *"Ki le'michya shlechani Elokim lifneichem,"* because God has sent me ahead of you to save lives.[63]

Yosef could have easily thrown fuel on the fire and been harsh

62   *Bereishis* 44:30.
63   Ibid., 45:5.

with them by saying that they *should* feel bad for what they did to him. Instead, he goes just the other way. He tries to assuage his brothers' feelings. He says to them, "Don't worry, don't feel guilty, because after all *"le'michya shelachani Elokim lifneichem,"*[64] God has sent me for the good, to save lives.

Our Rabbis tell us that Yosef is Yosef Hatzaddik, Yosef the righteous one.

Yosef is Yosef Hatzaddik because he repaid his brothers with goodness and kindness despite the fact that they acted improperly towards him. Yosef, even if he cannot fully see the bigger picture, knows that there *is* a bigger picture. *"Ki le'michya shelachani Elokim lifneichem."* Yosef understands that it is God who is in control and it is God who has sent him. This is such an important lesson, which we are to learn from Yosef. One has to believe that through all the trials and tribulations, through all of life's difficulties, there is also the good, and God is arranging for a brighter future. If someone acts badly to us, it is part of God's plan.

Parshas Vayigash is generally read around the time of the Fast of Asarah B'Teves. On the tenth of Teves, Nevuchadnezzar, king of Bavel (Babylonia), put a siege around Jerusalem, thereby marking the beginning of the end of the first Beis Hamikdash. How important is this fast? This fast is so important that were Asarah B'Teves to fall on a Shabbos, we would fast even on Shabbos. While in practice the Rabbis arrange the calendar so that this won't occur, in theory it could — something that could never happen for any other fasts, except for Yom Kippur. In fact, sometimes the month of Kislev is thirty days just so that Asarah B'Teves will fall on a Sunday.

Why is Asarah B'Teves so important?

The Chasam Sofer, *zt"l*, on his commentary to the *Selichos* for Asarah B'Teves, explains that it was on Asarah B'Teves that very first year that the following two events occurred. First, the siege was placed around Jerusalem. Second, the Heavenly Tribunal was convened by God. It was on this day that it was determined that the

---

64   Ibid., 45:5.

Beis Hamikdash would be destroyed. The Chasam Sofer points out that each and every year that the Beis Hamikdash is not rebuilt, it is as if, unfortunately, it is destroyed that year. Therefore, every year on Asarah B'Teves they reconvene the Heavenly Tribunal to determine if the Beis Hamikdash is going to be rebuilt that year — or not.

The Chasam Sofer cites the following very interesting difference as to when one would fast on Shabbos and when one would not. He brings two cases from the realm of *taanis yachid*, when an individual accepts a fast upon himself. For example, if someone has the practice of fasting on a *yahrzeit* and the *yahrzeit* falls on a Shabbos, the law says that one would not fast on Shabbos. Why? This is called an *aveilus yeshanah*, a mourning of the past. We would not allow a mourning of the past to dispel and take away from the sanctity of Shabbos and the specialty of the day. However, if, God forbid, a person has a disturbing dream on Friday night, then they are permitted to have a *taanis chalom*, they are permitted to fast on Shabbos day because this is not considered an *aveilus*, mourning, of the past. It is, rather, an *aveilus* of the moment. An *aveilus* of the moment would enable a person to have this emotion outweigh the *oneg* which normally accompanies Shabbos, thereby permitting him to fast on Shabbos.

How is this connected to Asarah B'Teves?

As the Chasam Sofer pointed out, on Asarah B'Teves every year there is a judgment as to whether the Beis Hamikdash is going to be rebuilt that year. Fasting on Asarah B'Teves is not simply commemorating an ancient *aveilus*, an old mourning. Rather, it is something current as well! Therefore, if Asarah B'Teves were to fall on Shabbos, we would fast on Shabbos just as we would fast for a *taanis chalom* on Shabbos day.

Each of us should learn the lesson of Yosef and realize that even our being in *galus* is not simply punitive in nature. It is also rehabilitative. Even in the *galus*, there is good, which will bring us out of the *galus*. There is *matzmiach yeshuah*, light at the end of the tunnel. Help and salvation are on the way. As Yosef was able to see the positive and the good, this is what we must learn as well.

We must learn from *Parshas Vayigash* from Yosef, and from Asarah B'Teves. What are we to learn? We are to learn that there is that bigger picture. Even though someone may act towards us in an unbrotherly, hateful manner, our job is to respond with kindness. As we know, *sinas chinam* destroyed the Beis Hamikdash; *chesed* (even when the recipients don't "deserve it") can help rebuild it.

VAYECHI
PASSION CHANNELED

Yaakov blesses his children prior to his passing, as the Torah tells us *"ish asher kevirchaso beirach osam,"*[65] each one in accordance with his (individual) blessing did Yaakov bless them. At first glance, it is difficult to see the blessing which he gives to Shimon and Levi when he says *"arur apam ki az,"*[66] literally cursed is their rage for it is mighty. What kind of blessing begins with the word "cursed"?! Yaakov continues, *"Achalkeim be'Yaakov va'afitzeim be'Yisrael,"*[67] I will divide them [Shimon and Levi] throughout Yaakov and I will disperse them in Israel.

Our Rabbis understand that Yaakov is referring to the incident[68] whereby they initiated and executed the killing of the town of Shechem. Yaakov understands that something needs to be done in order to improve their character. Rashi reveals what *Chazal* comment on this verse: Yaakov directed them to become teachers of Torah.

---

65   Ibid., 49:28.
66   Ibid., 49:7.
67   Ibid.
68   Ibid., 34:25-26.

In his *sefer Emes Le'Yaakov*, Rabbi Yaakov Kamenetsky, *zt"l* explains this idea in a unique and powerful way. Shimon and Levi demonstrated an incredible passion and determination for that which they saw was right. *All* the brothers were troubled by that which had occurred to Dina, however, it was *only* Shimon and Levi who stood up and took the initiative in order to rectify the situation.

Think about it.

What do we want for our children in the classroom? We want teachers with passion.

What do we want for our community? We want leaders who are going to be troubled when there are events taking place which demand an appropriate response.

Yaakov is smart. He teaches us insightful parenting. He teaches us, on the one hand, that one has to at times channel a certain character trait, found in a child, and make sure that it goes in the right direction. This is in keeping with the verse in *Mishlei*, "*Chanoch la'na'ar al pi darko*"[69] — educate the child in accordance with his or her nature. What is the continuation of this verse? "*Gam ki yazkin lo yasur mimena*" — for when he ages, he won't leave it.

The Vilna Gaon explains that if you try to stifle the child in his youth, you may be successful in the short-term; the child will be obedient and listen. However, as soon as the child will be on his own, he will revert to his true nature. Therefore, what does Yaakov do? He keeps their passion and channels it for their descendants to become teachers and leaders within the Jewish community.

Yaakov, however, goes even further. He understands that the brothers also possessed the trait of *achrayus*, responsibility. A teacher could certainly say regarding himself, "*Ani es nafshi eshmor*," I will take care of myself, my own soul, my own obligation for studying Torah. Instead, he prepares and devotes many, many hours for the perpetuation and continuity of the *tzibbur* (community). Shimon and Levi are the ones who take the *achrayus*, the responsibility.

---

69   *Mishlei* 22:6.

The *gemara*[70] cites a verse from the Book of *Daniel*, whereby Daniel is speaking about the great light which God will bestow upon those who are deserving at the time of the Final Redemption. "*Ve'ha-maskilim yazhiru kezohar ha-rakia,*"[71] and the wise will shine like the radiance of the firmament. The verse continues, "*U'matzdikei ha-rabim ka'kochavim le'olam va'ed,*" and those who make the many righteous will shine like the stars forever and ever.

The Talmud explains that *ha-maskilim* refers to both judges who judge truthfully and the *gaba'ay tzedakah*, who collect money for the *tzibbur*. Who are the *matzdikei ha-rabim*, who will shine like the stars forever and ever? These are *melamdei tinokos*, the teachers of children! The teachers of children are the ones, who are, please God, paving the way for the perpetuation of our people. These are the ones who take responsibility not only for themselves but for our collective future.

Each of us needs to be *matzdikei ha-rabim*, enabling others to become *tzaddikim*. Each and every person has to ask himself a very basic question: What am I doing for the community today? It is nice that when you pray, you pray for others as well. The very language of prayer — in the plural — indicates that you are praying for others as well. That is important, but what do you do for the *rabim*?

The answer has to be that I support institutions of Torah. I support institutions of *chesed*. I am part of the Jewish mission. I am contributing to it with my time, energy and money. I have to recognize that there is this Yissachar and Zevulun partnership, which is found in *Parshas Vayechi* as well.[72] If I cannot do it, I will nevertheless ensure that it will be done. In this way, I too will become a partner in the *matzdikei ha-rabim*.

Yaakov is such an insightful parent. He teaches us the following very important point: to channel our courage and passion to be used to benefit the rest of the community.

May we learn and become strengthened on this *Shabbos Chazak* from Yaakov's last will and testament to identify and use our talents, skills, resources, and energy, to help each other become *tzaddikim*.

---

70   *Bava Basra* 8b.
71   *Daniel* 12:3.
72   See Rashi on *Bereishis* 49:13.

SHEMOS
BROTHERLY LOVE

In the beginning of the second chapter of *Sefer Shemos*, the Torah describes how Moshe's mother, after successfully hiding Moshe for three months, has no choice but to take him and put him into a special basket on the Nile River.[73] Pharoah's daughter finds the baby, and, as the verse states, *"Va'tiftach va'tireihu es ha-yeled,"*[74] she opened the basket and she saw him (the child). The Torah refers to Moshe as *"ha-yeled,"* the child. The same verse continues, *"Ve'hinei na'ar boche,"* and behold a youth is crying.

How are we to understand that the Torah refers to Moshe both as a *yeled* and as a *na'ar*? Rashi cites the opinion of both *Shemos Rabbah*[75] and the *gemara* in *Sotah*,[76] both of which say *"kolo ke'na'ar,"* that his voice was like that of a youth. In the *gemara*, this is the opinion of Rabbi Yehuda.

Rabbi Nechemia points out that if this is correct then "You have made Moshe to have a significant blemish: As a baby he had a voice

---

73   See *Shemos* 2:2-3.
74   *Shemos* 2:6.
75   1:21.
76   12b.

which was much too mature for his age." Instead, he explains that one can feel the deep emotional pain which Moshe's mother must have felt as she put her baby into this basket, not knowing what would become of her child. She therefore constructed a little bit of a *chupah* in the basket, saying, "Perhaps I will not be privileged to be there at his *chupah* because he is not going to survive this experience." So she made him a *chupas ne'urim*. In other words, the word *na'ar* in this verse, explains Rabbi Nechemia, refers to that *chupah* which Yocheved put over him in the basket.

The *Midrash Abkir*[77] understands the verse to read as follows: Batya, Pharoah's daughter, opens up the basket, "*Va'tireihu es ha-yeled*," and she sees the child. Who is the child? Moshe. The verse continues, "*ve'hinei na'ar boche*," and she hears a youth crying. The youth crying, however, is not coming from the basket. Rather, the youth crying is Aharon, Moshe's brother, who is standing nearby. As soon as his baby brother is taken, not knowing what is going to happen to him, Aharon begins to cry. When Batya saw the baby and heard the cries of his older brother, she realized the attachment they had for one another. Rav Yaakov Rabinowitz, *shlita*, in his *sefer Yemin Yaakov*, points out that when one brother cries for another, the redemption begins.

Our redemption begins in our *parsha*, when we find Moshe Rabbeinu resisting the position which God offers him. God offers Moshe a position which is almost irresistible. Moshe resists for a week's time, and ultimately comes out with his final reason, "*Shelach na be'yad tishlach*,"[78] send who You should send, meaning send Aharon. "I have been away from the people for sixty years," says Moshe. "Aharon has been there with them, in the trenches, for sixty years. Aharon is Your man."

At the end of this long exchange, God finally says to Moshe, "Moshe, *you* are My man, but don't worry about Aharon. When Aharon sees you, '*ve'ra'acha ve'samach be'libo*,'[79] he is going to be exceedingly

77   Brought down in the *Yalkut Shimoni* and cited in the commentary of the *Chizkuni*.
78   *Shemos* 4:13.
79   Ibid., 4:14.

happy for you." Only at this point does Moshe acquiesce and assume the mantle of leadership and responsibility on behalf of the Jewish nation.

We know that *sinas achim* brought the Jewish nation down to Egypt and led us into servitude. In our *parsha* we learn how to undo this cycle. The rectification of this sin is, of course, its opposite: one brother going out of his way and willing to sacrifice for the other.

The *Braisa*, in the sixth chapter of *Avos*, teaches us that the Torah is acquired in forty-eight ways with which a person has to build his character. One of those ways is *"nosei be'ol im chaveiro,"* sharing your fellow's yoke, meaning feeling your friend's pain and doing whatever you can to help. The truth is that it is relatively easy to feel the pain of another person because our pity and empathy are aroused in such situations. However, *"ve'ra'acha ve'samach be'libo,"*[80] to be genuinely happy for the success of the next person, is something which is exceedingly difficult to attain. One has to strive to reach the level of *simchah* as if it were his or her own.

Think about it. When someone wins the lottery, of course you are happy for him. Deep down, however, you might wish that it was *you* who had won the lottery. Nevertheless, when you think it through you realize that Hashem wanted it, specifically, for that person. Then, you can be genuinely happy for him.

Another example: When two people are competing for the same position, and there can only be one winner, it is hard for the loser to be a "good loser." However, the *Mishnah* asks that we be genuinely happy for the "other guy." This is not an easy task, and it explains why the Torah compliments Moshe and Aharon for their incredible devotion one towards another.

What a powerful idea we are taught in *Parshas Shemos*. Our redemption does not begin when Moshe says, "Yes, I will take the position." Rather, the redemption begins when Moshe's brother cries for

---

80   *Shemos* 4:14.

him. When we care for each other, feel for each other, cry for each other and rejoice for each other — that is the start of the process of our redemption. What an appropriate beginning to *Sefer Shemos*, *Sefer Hageulah*, the book of our redemption.

VA'ERA
NO SHORTCUTS

In the opening of *Parshas Va'era*, God instructs Moshe to inform the Jewish people as to the master plan of their redemption from Egypt:

לָכֵן אֱמֹר לִבְנֵי-יִשְׂרָאֵל, אֲנִי יְהוָה, וְהוֹצֵאתִי אֶתְכֶם מִתַּחַת סִבְלֹת מִצְרַיִם, וְהִצַּלְתִּי אֶתְכֶם מֵעֲבֹדָתָם; וְגָאַלְתִּי אֶתְכֶם בִּזְרוֹעַ נְטוּיָה, וּבִשְׁפָטִים גְּדֹלִים. וְלָקַחְתִּי אֶתְכֶם לִי לְעָם, וְהָיִיתִי לָכֶם לֵאלֹהִים; וִידַעְתֶּם, כִּי אֲנִי יְהוָה אֱלֹהֵיכֶם, הַמּוֹצִיא אֶתְכֶם, מִתַּחַת סִבְלוֹת מִצְרָיִם.

Therefore, say to the Children of Israel, I am Hashem. **I shall take you out** from under the burdens of Egypt, and **I shall rescue you** from their service. **I shall redeem you** with an outstretched arm and with great judgments. **I shall take you** to me for a people, and I shall be a God to you.[81]

---

81   Ibid., 6:6-7.

According to the *Talmud Yerushalmi*, these four expressions of redemption are the source for our drinking four cups of wine on the night of the Pesach Seder. Each cup represents a step in the right direction.

What event does each of the four phrases refer to?

The Netziv in his commentary understands that *ve'hotzeisi* refers to the stage of the plague of *arov* (wild animals), at which point the back-breaking servitude ceased. *Bnei Yisrael*, however, remained enslaved until *vehitzalti* — the plague of *barad* (hail) discussed at the end of *Parshas Va'era*. Then comes *makkas bechoros* (the plague of the first-born), which according to the Netziv represents *ve'ga'alti*. *Ve'lakachti*, subsequently, takes place at Sinai.

The Seforno in his commentary understands *ve'hotzeisi* to mean that as soon as the plagues began, the servitude was diminished. *Ve'hitzalti* — I will save you — happens when *Bnei Yisrael* reach the borders on their way out of Egypt. *Ve'ga'alti* — I will redeem you — takes place by the drowning of the Egyptians at the Red Sea. Finally, *ve'lakachti* occurs at Sinai.

What we see from these interpretations is that redemption was a step-by-step process, and we are to give appreciation for each step along the way.

This idea is comparable to the long list of *Dayeinu*s at the Pesach Seder. *Dayeinu*, literally, means it would have been sufficient. The statements we recite are not to be understood at face value. Take, for example, the *dayeinu* of "*ilu keirvanu lifnei Har Sinai*," if God would only have brought us to Har Sinai, and not given us the Torah, "*dayeinu*" — that would have been sufficient. Can we really mean that it would have been sufficient simply to arrive at Har Sinai and *not* receive the Torah?! The whole goal is to receive the Torah! The point of the song is that each step that is mentioned would have been sufficient in order to warrant praise and thanksgiving to God. At *each* step along the way, we are to say, "Thank you, God, for *this*." Not that this is all we wanted. No! We want the ultimate. We want to get the Torah, we want to come into Eretz

Yisrael. However, we are to be appreciative that each step in the process is significant.

The twenty-second chapter of *Tehillim* begins "*La'menatzei'ach al ayeles ha-shachar.*" The *gemara* in *Megillah*[82] understands *ayeles ha-shachar* as referring to the morning star. The *Talmud Yerushalmi* in *Yoma*[83] asks how we are to understand the redemption of the Jewish people and explains that it is like the morning star — transition from night to day. The prophet *Michah* says, "*Ki eishev ba'choshech Hashem or li,*"[84] when I sit in the dark, God is my light. His point is that just as it would be injurious to the eye to go from darkness to light in a sudden fashion, so too the redemptive process cannot go from one extreme to the other in one instance. The Netziv notes that just as the Jewish people went from the extreme of slavery to receiving the Torah via a process of various stages, so too will be the final redemption of the Jewish people.

We see this process unfolding before our own eyes. With all the problems and with all the criticism one may have of the State of Israel, we must pause each and every day and say, "Wow! This is the land for which our ancestors and our grandparents prayed and poured out their hearts. We have the privilege of being there, of living there, of developing it. We have the opportunity to create out of the Land of Israel a land of Torah!" We are witnessing the process of redemption. Sure, we would like it to happen quicker. The *geulah*, however, comes *kim'a kim'a*, in gradual fashion. We are to be appreciative and we are to give thanksgiving for each and every step along this process.

Finally, each individual should realize that everyone has their *peckel*, their individual challenge of *yetzias Mitzrayim*. Each person was put on the planet for a unique purpose in order to overcome struggles, as well as various trials and difficulties. The redemptive process of the individual does not happen overnight. It is a pro-

---

82 15b.
83 *Yerushalmi Yoma* 3:2.
84 *Michah* 7:8.

cess. It requires work. After all, *"Ki adam la'amel yulad,"*[85] man is born to labor. The Dubno Maggid relates the dictum of King David, *"Kos yeshu'os essa,"* I lift up a cup, literally, to say thank you to God, *"u've'shem Hashem ekra,"*[86] but I am still calling out for more. A Jew has to realize that there is always the opportunity for personal growth.

This is precisely what the Rambam writes at the end of chapter 10 of the Laws of *Brachos*:

כְּלָלוֹ שֶׁל דָּבָר: לְעוֹלָם יִצְעַק אָדָם עַל הֶעָתִיד לָבוֹא, וִיבַקֵּשׁ
רַחֲמִים; וְיִתֵּן הוֹדָיָה עַל שֶׁעָבַר, וְיוֹדֶה וִישַׁבַּח כְּפִי כֹּחוֹ.

> The rule is that man should always cry out for the future and ask for mercy, while at the same time giving thanksgiving for that which transpired and acknowledging and praising God according to his ability.[87]

The four expressions of redemption found at the beginning of *Parshas Va'era* carry a very important lesson both nationally and personally for each and every one of us. It is a process. As a people and as individuals, we need to go through the process, thanking God for each step along the way, until, please God, we are each privileged to arrive at our ultimate national and personal redemption.

---

85 *Iyov* 5:7.
86 *Tehillim* 116:13.
87 *Rambam, Mishneh Torah, Hilchos Brachos* 10:26.

BO
EVERY DAY IS A MIRACLE

The Jewish nation was born out of miracles. The enslaved people witnessed the wonders of Hashem in Egypt in conjunction with the ten plagues. They were escorted out of Egypt with the Divine cloud by day and with a pillar of fire by night. They walked through the water, on dry land, in the Yam Suf. They witnessed the Egyptians drowning. At Mara, the bitter waters turned sweet by throwing a bitter tree into them. The daily miraculous ration of *mohn* nourished the Jewish people, but rotted if kept overnight, except on Shabbos when Friday's double portion retained its freshness. The menorah in the *Mishkan* was fashioned miraculously out of fire.[88] For forty years, the Jewish nation was surrounded by constant miracles. The great significance of these miracles, notes the last Ramban in our *parsha*[89], is to impress upon the Jewish nation the close personal relationship which Hashem has with *Bnei Yisrael*. His *hashgachah pratis*, Divine intervention, His concern for their welfare, is the cornerstone upon which the Jewish nation is founded.

---

88   See Rashi on *Shemos* 25:40.

89   *Ramban* 13:16.

Sadly, but realistically, the nature of man is to forget. And it doesn't take long. Not only do later generations forget the impact of ancient historical miracles, but even the one to whom the miracle occurred is wont to forget, unless he works hard at remembering what happened. Case in point: Rabbi Rachmiel Krohn, in his *sefer Ve'talmudo Be'yado*, shares another example regarding the relative ease of individuals to forget miracles which occur to them. He notes that while Moshe successfully prays for the recovery of his sister, Miriam, when she has *tzara'as* (leprosy), he does not pray on his own behalf to have his speech impediment cured. Why not? Moshe wanted to always remember the miracle, whereby he experienced an angel moving and directing his infant hand to the hot coals rather than to the alluring gold.[90] This is what saved his life. Had his speech defect been removed, Moshe too may have forgotten the miracle.

If the direct recipient of the miracle is prone to forget it, all the more so their descendants and future generations!

How can we prevent this from happening, and thereby keep the memory of ancient miracles fresh in the minds of present and future generations?

Ramban explains that the primary purpose of many *mitzvos* is *zecher le'yetzias Mitzrayim*, to remember the exodus from Egypt and its accompanying miracles and wonders. To offset the heresy that Hashem is removed from the activities of mankind, Hashem suspends nature and has us incorporate His miraculous involvement as an integral part of many *mitzvos*. Thus, our donning *tefillin*, putting *mezuzos* on our doors, the many prohibitions of *chametz* coupled with the mitzvah of eating matzah, all of which are contained in *Parshas Bo*, help keep the memory of the miracle alive. Also, our annual migration to the *sukkah*, the Torah explains, is *"le'ma'an yeidu doroseichem,"*[91] so that your generations will know that millions of people were fed, clothed and sustained miraculously for forty years in a desert environment.

---

90   *Yalkut Shimoni, Shemos* 166.
91   *Vayikra* 23:43.

Moreover, while Hashem does perform miracles, it is not His desire to perform open miracles regularly. On the contrary, it is the way of Hashem, most often, to minimize the extent of the miracle. Thus, technically, notes the Ramban in *Parshas Noach*[92], even many arks the size of Noach's ark would not suffice to house all the animals and their provisions for a year's time. Yet, having Noach build a relatively large ark couches the miraculous within the natural order of things.

The Steipler, *zt"l*, in his *sefer Chayei Olam*, suggests an interesting reason why miracles were the order of the day at the time of the foundation of our people. At that time, they needed to learn the very important lesson of our connection to Hashem. However, the presence of open miracles diminishes the free will of man and further, having witnessed open miracles, the level of expectation and accountability for man is raised. As a result, even smaller infractions are treated more seriously. Given the nature of man to forget miracles, and the fact that they make us more responsible, miracles themselves only serve to create obstacles for us!

Let us close with a very moving story which we find in the *gemara Taanis*.[93]

The Rabbis teach that it once happened that all Israel went up to Jerusalem for a pilgrim festival. Due to a terrible drought, there was not enough water for them to drink. Nakdimon ben Gurion, a very wealthy Jew, approached a Roman with the following proposal. "Lend me twelve wells of water for the pilgrims' use," he said to the Roman, "and I will give you back twelve wells of water. If I do not return the water to you, I will give you twelve talents of silver (an especially large amount of money)." Nakdimon then set a time and a date for the repayment of the water.

When the deadline arrived and the rains had not yet fallen, the Roman sent a message to Nakdimon in the morning stating, "Send me either the water or the money you owe me." Nakdimon sent back

---

92   *Ramban* 6:19.
93   19b.

the following reply, "I still have time. The whole day is mine to repay the water." In the afternoon, the wealthy Roman sent him another message, "Send me either the water or the money you owe me." Once again, Nakdimon sent the message back to him, "I still have time in the day to repay the water."

In the late afternoon, the Roman sent to him again, "Send me either the water or the money you owe me." Nakdimon sent back to him, "I still have time in the day to repay the water." At this point, the Roman mocked him saying, "No rains have fallen the entire year and you expect the rains to fall during this short time before the end of the day?!" The Roman then entered the bathhouse[94] in joy, confident that Nakdimon would have to pay him the huge sum of money.

Meanwhile, as the Roman entered the bathhouse, Nakdimon entered the Beis Hamikdash in desperation. He wrapped himself in his garment and stood in prayer. He said before Hashem, "Master of the Universe, it is clearly known before You that I did not do this (undertake to provide water for the pilgrims) for my personal honor nor did I do so for the honor of my father's house. Rather, I did it for Your honor so that the water would be available to the pilgrims to enjoy the festival, Your holiday." Immediately, the sky became overcast with clouds and rain fell until the twelve wells borrowed from the Roman filled beyond the level where they had started.

As the Roman emerged from the bathhouse, Nakdimon emerged from the Beis Hamikdash. When they encountered one another, Nakdimon said to him, "Aha! Now *you* give me the money for the surplus water, which I have now given you beyond the amount you gave to me." The Roman replied to him, "I know that God clearly altered His world by sending a rainstorm so late in the season solely on your account. Nevertheless, you still owe me the money. The sun has already set, so the rains have fallen in *my* possession, past the deadline."

Nakdimon then re-entered the Temple. He wrapped himself in

---

94   The Maharsha notes that by going into the bathhouse, the Roman was further mocking Nakdimon. How so? The Jews did not even have enough water to drink. And yet, this Roman had enough even to bathe.

his garment once again and stood in prayer. He said, "Ribono shel Olam, Master of the Universe, make it known that You have beloved ones in Your universe." Immediately, the clouds dispersed and the sun shone through, thereby demonstrating that the day had not yet ended, and that Nakdimon had indeed repaid the water on time.

This powerful story helps us appreciate the fact that there are two types of miracles. The open, revealed miracles such as the splitting of the sea don't happen very often. What about regular life? In the *brachah* of *Modim*, which we recite thrice daily in the *amidah*, we say "*Al neesecha she'be'chol yom imanu*" — We thank You, Hashem, for Your miracles which are with us daily. This includes the natural phenomena around us such as the burning of oil.[95] It also includes the survival of the State of Israel, surrounded by multitudes of unfriendly Arabs. It includes, as well, His direct *hashgachah pratis*, His direct involvement in our personal and communal lives as the many *mitzvos* of *zecher le'yetzias Mitzrayim* proclaim.

May we ever be appreciative of the manifold miracles, which surround us at all times.

---

95   As Rabbi Chanina said, "As God empowered and endowed oil with the ability to burn, so too can He cause vinegar to burn."

BESHALACH
NO PAIN, NO GAIN

The Torah tells us at the very beginning of *Parshas Beshalach*, *"Va'yikach Moshe es atzmos Yosef imo,"*[96] Moshe takes
with him, at the time of the Exodus from Egypt, literally,
the bones (or the remains) of Yosef. This was in accordance
with Yosef's request of the Jewish people, by which he had them
swear that when God will remember them, "please bring up my
bones from here [Egypt] with you."[97] Moshe is the one who takes
upon himself the responsibility to fulfill this request.

The *Midrash Rabbah*[98] teaches that the verse from *Mishlei*, *"Chacham lev yikach mitzvos,"*[99] the man with the wise heart acquires *mitzvos*, applies particularly to Moshe. The *midrash* explains the context.
Immediately before the Exodus, the Children of Israel were busy
gathering valuables from the Egyptians, as God had told them, "Ask
the Egyptians for their gold and their silver (and their clothes)."[100]

---

96   *Shemos* 13:19.
97   *Bereishis* 50:25; *Shemos* 13:19.
98   20:19.
99   *Mishlei* 10:8.
100   See *Shemos* 11:2 and 12:35.

The *midrash* is lauding Moshe — while the rest of the Jews were gathering the gold, Moshe was doing a mitzvah.

One can very well argue, however, that what the Jews were doing was also a mitzvah! They were fulfilling the promise that God made to Avraham, *"Ve'acharei chein yeitzu bi'rechush gadol,"*[101] they would leave with great wealth. Why, then, does the *midrash* favor Moshe?

The *midrash* teaches us that not all *mitzvos* are created equal. Of course, all *mitzvos* are extremely important. However, in terms of God's ultimate accounting system, the *mitzvos* which are more challenging and difficult and, perhaps, on the surface, less attractive, are the ones for which a person receives greater reward.

If one has a choice between searching for the bones of Yosef or taking the loot of Egypt, most people would take the more attractive mitzvah of going after the money. Moshe realized that the less attractive mitzvah of carrying the bones would be neglected, and understood as well the special importance of bringing a *tzaddik* to his final burial in the Land of Israel. The *midrash* concludes that Moshe was rewarded with the privilege of having God Himself bury him when it came time for him to pass on.

The most significant idea which emerges from this *midrash* is the importance of *le'fum tza'ara agra*, in proportion to the exertion is the reward. When this idea is taught in *Avos Di'Rabi Nosson,*[102] Rabbi Yishmael adds that it is better for a person to do one difficult mitzvah than to do a hundred easy ones.

We find this idea very powerfully expressed in the *gemara Sanhedrin.*[103] In the *Eishes Chayil* which we sing prior to the recitation of *kiddush* on Friday night, we conclude with the following message: *"Sheker ha'chein ve'hevel ha'yofi isha yiras Hashem he tishallal,"*[104] grace is false and beauty is vain but a God-fearing woman is she who is to be praised. Aside from the literal understanding of this

---

101 *Bereishis* 15:14.
102 Ch. 3.
103 20a.
104 *Mishlei* 31:30.

verse, which is important, note the way the Talmud understands this as well.

What was King Solomon referring to by a "God-fearing woman should be praised"? The *gemara* explains that this refers to the generation of Rabbi Yehuda son of Rebbe Ila'i. Due to their extreme poverty, six of his disciples would cover themselves with one blanket. This is the way they studied Torah in the wintertime, without any heat. And yet, they would continue to study Torah. They were willing to put themselves out.

Today, Torah has never been more accessible. This is due to the incredible amount of publishing in any and every language as well as to the innovations of technology and the accessibility of Torah on the internet. However, things are not so simple. All is not perfect with the new accessibility of Torah. As pointed out by the Netziv,[105] there are two types of Torah study. The Torah says, *"Ya'arof ka'matar likchi tizal ka'tal imrasi."*[106] God says to the Jewish nation, "My teaching shall drip like the rain and My utterance shall flow like the dew." Torah is called *matar*, rain, as well as *tal*, dew. Rashi says that everyone loves *tal*, dew, because it provides an initial amount of freshness, and carries with it no annoyance to people whatsoever. On the other hand, rain is less desired, as it can be an inconvenience for travelers and others. How then can Torah be called *matar*, rain, knowing full well the negative connotation which this term holds? Is Hashem, *chas v'shalom*, really telling us that the Torah, or parts thereof, can be undesirable?

The Netziv explains that there are two kinds of Torah. There is the rain and the dew. There is the little *vertel*, the nice little idea, which everyone likes. This, explains the Netziv, is the Torah of dew. The rain is the more difficult form of Torah study in which a person has to discipline himself — the *amalah* and the *yegiah*, the exertion and the effort, in the study of Torah. Unless a person actually puts in the time and effort, he or she is not really going to attain the essence and the heart of Torah study.

---

105 At the beginning of *Parshas Ha'azinu*.
106 *Devarim* 32:2.

Moshe strove higher to do a higher level of mitzvah. We should strive higher to do a higher level of Torah learning. We should work hard at it. The principle holds true for all *mitzvos*.

The holiday of Tu B'Shevat appropriately falls out around the time when we read *Parshas Beshalach*. Tu B'Shevat represents the fact that the sap is rising in the trees and that the fruits will be coming and getting rejuvenated. So too, at this time, we are to remind ourselves not to be lazy in our performance of the *mitzvos*. We are not to be satisfied with our performance of only those *mitzvos* which are easy for us. On the contrary, we should work hard to do the hard ones as well. Take, for example, the more difficult task of getting to *shul* on time for *minyan*. What can one do to break the habit of getting there a little late? He can set the clock a few minutes earlier, and thereby improve his chances of making it on time. It will take a little bit of effort on his part, but it will be worthwhile for him in the long run. Similarly, in regard to breaking the habit of not learning during the week, or of leaving *shul* early, or even of talking in *shul*.

This is what the Torah is communicating to us upon teaching that Moshe is praised "*chacham lev yikach mitzvos.*" We are all involved in *mitzvos*. It is time, however, to graduate from the easy ones and to start accepting upon ourselves those which are a little bit more difficult as well. *Hatzlachah Rabbah!*

YISRO
TEACH BY EXAMPLE

Prior to the revelation at Mount Sinai, Hashem told the Jewish people:

וְעַתָּה, אִם-שָׁמוֹעַ תִּשְׁמְעוּ בְּקֹלִי, וּשְׁמַרְתֶּם, אֶת-בְּרִיתִי--וִהְיִיתֶם לִי סְגֻלָּה מִכָּל-הָעַמִּים, כִּי-לִי כָּל-הָאָרֶץ. וְאַתֶּם תִּהְיוּ-לִי מַמְלֶכֶת כֹּהֲנִים, וְגוֹי קָדוֹשׁ.

And now, if you listen well to Me and observe My covenant, you will be to Me the most beloved treasure of all peoples for the entire land is Mine. [And then] you shall be to Me a kingdom of priests and a holy nation...[107]

What does it mean to be a *"mamleches kohanim,"* a kingdom of priests?

Rav Avraham, the son of the Rambam, explains that a priest is

---

107 *Shemos* 19:5-6.

the honored one, the paradigm, the example — he whom the rest of the people are to emulate. The priests, the *kohanim*, were thereby the teachers and the leaders of the nation. What the *kohein* is to the Jewish nation, the Jewish nation is to the rest of the world.

The prophet Yeshaya points out that we are to be an *or la'goyim*,[108] a light unto the nations. If one, indeed, looks at world history, God's *a priori* plan was that from Adam, everyone would believe in and follow God and live life accordingly. Unfortunately, already in the days of Adam's grandson, idolatry came into this world. God consequently destroyed the world in a great flood, and through Noach offered humanity a second chance. Unfortunately, with the sin of *dor haflagah* (the attempt to build the Tower of Bavel), once again mankind wasted its opportunity, and Hashem decided to try something different. His plan was to choose one man with whom He could entrust a very special lifestyle, and who would subsequently pass this lifestyle on to his family. Hashem would then build for Himself a nation from this family. At the very beginning of *Parshas Lech Lecha*, when God reveals His plan and His intention to Avraham, He says to Avraham, *"Ve'nivrechu becha kol mishpechos ha-adomah,"* through you all the families of the earth will be blessed.[109] They will learn from and emulate Avraham. As a result, their way of life will become enhanced.

In *Devarim Rabbah*,[110] a story is told of the famous Rabbi Shimon ben Shetach. He once purchased a donkey from an Arab. When his students picked up the donkey on his behalf, they found a precious jewel suspended around the neck of the animal. They said to their teacher, citing from the tenth chapter of Proverbs, *"Birkas Hashem he ta'ashir,"*[111] it is the blessing of Hashem which causes one to become wealthy. They said, "Rebbe, it is your lucky day. You hit the jackpot. Look at this jewel around the neck of the animal." Reb Shimon ben Shetach answered them, "I only purchased a donkey. I did not pur-

---

108 *Yeshaya* 49:6.
109 *Bereishis* 12:3.
110 3:3.
111 *Mishlei* 10:22.

chase this jewel. It must be a mistake." He then returned the jewel to the Arab. The Arab, in turn, proclaimed out loud, obviously very overwhelmed, *"Baruch Hashem Elokei Shimon ben Shetach,"* Blessed is the God of Shimon ben Shetach.

This is the goal. A Jew is to live a life such that the people all around him recognize the special manner in which the Jewish people conduct themselves.

Rav Dessler, *zt"l*, writes[112], "Just because I am in pain, the other person does not have to suffer." For example, a person may have had a hard day at the office. However, that should not mean that one's children or one's spouse must suffer the consequences. This requires enormous self-control on the part of an individual. It also takes a person who treats each and every human being, Jew and non-Jew, with dignity.

There is a famous story[113] about a Catholic nun from Monsey, New York. She once remarked that people on the street of that largely Orthodox neighborhood did not bother to greet her. There were even some who mumbled derogatory remarks under their breath. However, there was one exception. A small man with a gray beard would greet her with a smiling Good morning every day. This man was none other than Rav Yaakov Kamenetsky, *zt"l*, one of the greatest Torah sages of our time.

This is an incredibly powerful concept. The Jew has enormous potential to influence the world in a positive way. The Torah tells us, *"Ve'ra'u kol amei ha'aretz ki shem Hashem nikra alecha ve'yaruh mi'meka,"* all the peoples of the earth will see that the name of God is proclaimed over you and they will revere you.[114]

The Gra asks, what does it mean that the nations of the world will, literally, *see* the name of God proclaimed upon the Jewish people? He understands the verse to mean that the nations of the world are going to see the way in which the Jew conducts himself. They are going to see a certain aura, a *feinkeit*, an *aidelkeit*, a spirituality which

---

112   *Michtav M'Elyahu* Vol. 4 pg. 245.
113   as told by Rabbi Yissachar Frand
114   *Devarim* 28:10.

is literally recognized on his face. As a result of this, they are going to "*yaruh oso.*" They are going to learn *yiras Shamayim.* They are going to learn the concept of fear and respect for God through the actions of the Jew.

It is a tall order. Accepting the Torah is a two-fold process. Not only are we to keep it, observe it, and live it, we are also to be those representatives of Torah who model it and teach it to the rest of the world.

Each year we read *Parshas Yisro* and we accept upon ourselves the Ten Commandments as well as the pledge of allegiance to follow the Torah. In so doing, we have to understand the responsibility borne by such acceptance, as we conclude the *davening* every day, "*Ve'haya Hashem le'melech al* **kol** *ha'aretz,*"[115] the day will come when *all* of mankind will proclaim Hashem as King. Rashi echoes this idea with his understanding of the verse "*Shema Yisrael Hashem Elokeinu Hashem echad.*"[116] The day will come, says Rashi, when Hashem, who is currently only *Elokeinu, our* God, will be *echad,* will be recognized throughout the entire world as the One and Only God.

May each and every one of us be privileged to hasten that day in coming.

---

115 *Zechariah* 14:9.
116 *Devarim* 6:4.

MISHPATIM
ELEVATOR OF KNOWLEDGE

arshas Mishpatim contains the basis and the foundation of the Jewish legal system. What is most fascinating is the fact that the *parsha* begins with the letter *vav*. The first verse is consequently read, "***Ve'eileh ha-mishpatim***"[117] — **And** these are the laws which you are to place before the people. It sounds as though *Parshas Mishpatim* is a continuation of the previous *parsha*, rather than its own portion.

How many extra letters are there in the Torah? The answer, of course, is none. The *parsha* could have begun, *Eileh ha'mishpatim*, these are the laws, and no one would have missed that additional *vav*. Rashi addresses this question by citing the *Mechilta*, which teaches, "*Mah ha-rishonim mi'Sinai af eilu mi'Sinai.*" The previous *parsha*, *Parshas Yisro*, was the *parsha* of the revelation at Mount Sinai and of the Ten Commandments. The Torah is teaching us, explains the *Mechilta*, that just as the Ten Commandments were given at Sinai, so too the laws listed in *Parshas Mishpatim* were given at Sinai as well.

---

117 *Shemos* 21:1.

What makes this principle so important that God added a letter to the Torah to teach it?

Consider a fascinating *midrash* in *Shemos Rabbah*[118] which expounds on the familiar verse from *Tehillim*, "*Kol Hashem ba'koach*,"[119] meaning, literally, that the voice of Hashem comes in power. The *midrash* proceeds to explain that the power in this verse is not the power of Hashem's voice. That would be impossible for man to endure. *Ba'koach*, rather, means that the voice of God comes in accordance with the capability — the *koach* — and the potential of each individual. This means that the young folk standing at Sinai understood the Ten Commandments one way, while those more mature understood it on a more sophisticated level. For example, the commandment which teaches "Thou shall not murder"[120] can be understood literally or it can be understood to prohibit embarrassing another person. Similarly, the commandment "Thou shall not steal" can be understood as not to kidnap, not to take the next person's property, or even not to give a false impression (known *halachically* as *geneivas da'as*).

Each one of the Ten Commandments can be understood in a variety of ways beyond its literal meaning, as well as on additional levels of comprehension. Similarly, the extra *vav* in our *parsha* teaches that while the *mishpatim* are often presented speaking to the lowest common denominator, they nevertheless contain many additional levels of application.

For example, the Torah teaches that one is to pay his workers in a timely fashion.[121] The Talmud in *Bava Metzia*[122] relates the following story concerning the extent of the application of this law. It is taught that Raba bar Rav Huna hired workers to transport barrels of wine on his behalf. The workers were negligent and broke some of the barrels. Thereupon, Raba bar Rav Huna confiscated their coats as

---

118 29:1.
119 *Tehillim* 29:4.
120 *Shemos* 20:13.
121 *Vayikra* 19:13.
122 83a.

collateral for the damages caused him. The workers then went to Rav, who ordered Raba to return their coats. When Raba questioned as to whether this was indeed the law, Rav answered in the affirmative, citing the verse from Proverbs, "*Le'ma'an teilech be'derech tovim*,"[123] in order that you may walk in the way of the good. When the workers further complained that they had worked all day long, they were poor, and they had not been compensated, Rav ordered Raba to pay them immediately. Once again, Raba questioned, "Is this indeed the law?" Rav again responded, "Yes," this time citing the second half of the above verse from Proverbs, "*Ve'orchos tzaddikim tishmor*," and keep the paths of the righteous.

This case teaches us the very important concept of *lifnim mi'shuras ha-din*, which means to go beyond the letter of the law. As the *vav* in *Ve'eileh ha'mishpatim* teaches us, laws have multiple levels of understanding and application. Rav understood that for a pious sage like Raba bar Rav Huna, the law was more stringent than for an average person.

A similar idea is taught regarding Shabbos in *Parshas Vayakhel*. The verse teaches: "*Yiyeh lachem kodesh*,"[124] it shall be holy for you. The Netziv understands this phrase as referring to each individual in accordance with his own station. Thus, explains the *Yerushalmi*, for the unlearned Jew, Shabbos is the day when he is careful not to lie. If you were to ask him during the week if his produce was tithed, you cannot rely upon his answer; he is suspect to lie. However, if you were to ask the same person on Shabbos, you can rely upon his answer because *eimas haShabbos alav*, the respect of the Shabbos is upon him.

This idea is taught in relation to an unlearned individual. It is clear, however, from here that the one who is more learned, the more observant Jew, will certainly not lie. For him, the verse teaches that his table talk on Shabbos has to rise above politics and sports to that of *divrei Torah*.

---

123 *Mishlei* 2:20.
124 *Shemos* 35:2.

Another example: In the first chapter of the Book of *Yehoshua*, we are taught that the Jew is to study Torah day and night, "*Ve'hagisa bo yomam va'lailah.*"[125] This is the ideal.

However, the Talmud in *Menachos*[126] teaches that there is, in fact, a bare minimum for the requirement of Torah study. Even simply reciting the *Shema*, morning and night, is sufficient. Says the Talmud, if a person says not just the opening line but at least the first paragraph of the *Shema*,[127] which itself contains verses of Torah, and he keeps in mind that this is his fulfillment of *talmud Torah* for the day, he has thereby fulfilled his obligation with the bare minimum. Is this the law for everyone? Certainly not; we should be striving to learn Torah as many hours as possible!

Ve'eileh ha-mishpatim teaches us that we are not meant to — or allowed to — strive for the minimum. The Torah applies to people differently at different stages in their lives. Often, it gives us the basics; it is up to us to constantly strive higher.

---

125 1:8.
126 99b.
127 *Devarim* 6:4-9.

TERUMAH
HOME AWAY FROM HOME

Parshas Terumah is the first of five *parshios* which deal with the details of the construction of the sanctuary, and indeed one of its *mitzvos* is the mitzvah of *"ve'asu li mikdash ve'shachanti be'socham,"*[128] they shall make a sanctuary for Me so that I may dwell amongst them.

At first, when *Bnei Yisrael* were traveling through the desert, this sanctuary took the form of a portable structure known as the *Mishkan*. Ultimately, we built the more permanent structure of the Beis Hamikdash. In actuality, we succeeded in building two, but failed in their maintenance. Please God, we shall succeed in building *and* maintaining the third and final Beis Hamikdash.

In conjunction with the mitzvah of building a sanctuary, consider a fascinating *gemara* found in *Brachos*.[129] Rabbi Yosi taught, "I was once walking on the road and I entered into a ruin, one of the ruins of Jerusalem, in order to pray. Eliyahu Hanavi (Elijah the Prophet) came and waited at the entrance of the ruin until I finished

---

128 *Shemos* 25:8.
129 3a.

my prayer. When I finished praying, he said to me, 'Peace be unto you, Rebbe.' I, in turn, responded to him, 'Peace be unto you, my Rebbe and teacher.' He then proceeded to ask me, 'What were you doing in the ruin?' I replied to him, 'I went in to pray.' He then told me, 'You should have prayed on the road.' I said to him, 'I was afraid that the passersby would interrupt and distract me.' He said, 'That being the case, it would have been better to pray a *tefillah ketzarah*, a short and abridged prayer, rather than go into the ruin because, practically speaking it is unsafe.'"[130]

The story continues. After cautioning Rabbi Yosi about entering a ruin, Eliyahu proceeds to ask him, "My son, what did you hear inside the ruin?" To which Rabbi Yosi replied, "I heard a *bas kol*, a heavenly voice, cooing like a dove and saying, 'Woe unto the children that because of their sins I have destroyed My House and burnt My Temple and I have exiled them amongst the nations.'" Eliyahu Hanavi then said to Rabbi Yosi, "I swear, this is not the only time when this heavenly voice says such things. Rather, it does so three times a day."

Moreover, Eliyahu continues, when the Jewish people enter their synagogues and study halls and answer in their prayers, "*Yehei shmei ha-gadol mevorach*,"[131] God responds positively, shaking His head and saying, "Fortunate is the king who is so praised in his home. Unfortunate for the king who has exiled his children, and woe to the children who have been exiled from their father's table."

Several interesting questions are asked about this *gemara*. First, why is the voice heard particularly in *this* ruin? Second, how is it that the voice in the ruin begins with "*Oy la'banim*," woe unto the sons, and God's response in the synagogues and study halls is "*Ashrei ha'melech*," fortunate is the king?

Rav Elyashiv, *zt"l*, in his *sefer Divrei Agada*, has an interesting understanding of this *gemara*. He suggests that this was not just any *churvah* (ruin) into which Rabbi Yosi entered. Rather, it was a syna-

---

130 Other reasons are listed there.
131 Which we know as *Yehei shmei Rabbah mevorach*.

gogue which had been destroyed and the people had not yet rebuilt it. Therefore, explains Rav Elyashiv, what the Talmud is teaching us is that God bemoans this fact and says "*Oy.*" "*Oy,*" cries God, "that you allow it to stay in ruins. "*Oy,*" says God, "if this were *your* home you would have rebuilt it and now unfortunately you do not." Thus, when we say to God in our prayers three times daily, "Restore the Temple," these are, in effect, empty words.[132] How so? We do not value enough even the *mikdash me'at*, the miniature temple, known as the synagogue!

The Talmud is teaching us that we must look upon the synagogue at least as well as we do upon our own homes. The same way that in our own homes we are constantly trying to make improvements, likewise the synagogue deserves our attention.

The Rambam, at the very end of *Hilchos Isurei Mizbei'ach*, writes that whatever we do in our service of God, we should try to do in the best manner possible. He concludes *Hilchos Isurei Mizbei'ach* in the following way:

וְהוּא הַדִּין,

לְכָל דָּבָר שֶׁהוּא לְשֵׁם הָאֵל הַטּוֹב--שֶׁיִּהְיֶה מִן הַנָּאֶה

הַטּוֹב: אִם בָּנָה בֵּית תְּפִלָּה, יִהְיֶה נָאֶה מִבֵּית יְשִׁיבָתוֹ.

> Similarly, this is the law that all of our directives which we focus towards God, should be from the best. If one builds a synagogue, it should be nicer than our own homes.[133]

The first point which we are being taught here is that of reverence towards the synagogue. When the synagogue is in disarray, the response of God is "*Oy.*" When, however, people respect the synagogue and come to the synagogue and they answer in a positive way

---

132 See *Kuzari* 2:24.

133 *Rambam, Mishneh Torah, Hilchos Isurei Mizbei'ach*, 7:11.

and they praise God, He responds in kind — "*Ashrei ha'melech*," fortunate is the king. This is the first step to our being able to have His Home, the future third Temple, dwell in our midst. We must show that we consider the miniature temple, our synagogues, to be most important. Then, and only then, God will see that we are ready for the responsibility which comes with having the Beis Hamikdash.

The second point which we are taught is that the significance of the synagogue goes beyond the *gashmius*, the physical conditions of the synagogue. What is happening in the *shul*? For example, when a stranger enters the synagogue is he welcomed and made to feel at home, or is he ignored and left to fend for himself? The answer to this question makes such a difference to the many Jews out there who are not yet so committed to *shul* attendance, and, from time to time, will find their way into a synagogue, for example, on a *yahrzeit* or for *Yizkor*. What a powerful opportunity it is! It is exactly what the Talmud is trying to teach us. When we, unfortunately, neglect the synagogue to the point of *churvah* (ruin), God responds with "*Oy*." If we understand that it is such a wonderful opportunity to spread the goodness, God responds with "*Ashrei*," fortunate is the king.

The Beis Hamikdash was a place of *chesed* (kindness). When Shlomo built the Beis Hamikdash, there was a special *sha'ar*, entranceway, for *chasanim* (bridegrooms). There was also a special entranceway for *aveilim* (mourners). The goal was that the joy and sorrow of others' lives should not be lost on us. We should empathize, celebrate and sympathize with one another, thereby bringing the Jewish people closer together. Similarly, this has to be the hallmark and the foundation of our synagogues. If our synagogues are *charev* in such a way that individuals pray inside the same building yet they do not form a unit, then the heavenly response is once again "*Oy*," woe to such people. If, however, they join together and help one another, then the response of Hashem is "*Ashrei ha'melech*," fortunate is the king.

We do not yet have the third Beis Hamikdash. The Talmud teaches us, however, a very important lesson. If we want to, in a very literal sense, implement the mitzvah of *"Ve'asu li mikdash ve'shachanti be'socham,"* then we should appreciate and elevate our synagogues so that they are physically and spiritually beautiful. If we do so, we will hasten the building of the true sanctuary, the Beis Hamikdash.

TETZAVEH
PARADISE FOUND

Have you ever wondered how it is possible that in the Holy of Holies there were the *kruvim*, the two cherub-like figures, which appear to be nothing less than graven images? After all, the Torah says explicitly in the second of the Ten Commandments that you are not to have a belief in another god and you are not to have a *pesel*, a graven image.[134]

Second, the Rabbis in the *gemara*[135] relate a striking occurrence. When the people would come on *aliyah la'regel, the pilgrimage to Jerusalem,* on Pesach, Shavuos, and Sukkos to the Beis Hamikdash, the *kohanim* would pull away the *paroches, the curtain in front of the Holy Ark,* and the people would see from a distance the *kruvim* which were *me'urim*, hugging each other. The *kohanim* would say to the people, "Look and see how beloved you are before God."

The *kruvim* were a barometer. Just as the affection of a husband and wife is demonstrated by their hugging each other, so too the *kruvim* show God's affection by hugging. At first glance, this seems

---

134 See *Shemos* 20:3-4 and *Devarim* 5:7-8.
135 *Yoma* 54b.

to be a violation of the element of *tznius*, modesty. There is certainly room for demonstrations of affection, but is this the most fitting place for it?

Rav Kook, *zt"l* suggests[136] a very novel interpretation. We are aware of the concept in international law known as extraterritorial. This means that the embassy of a foreign country is considered to be part of the foreign country, even though physically it is surrounded by its host country. Similarly, suggests Rav Kook, the Holy of Holies was an extraterritorial extension of Gan Eden. It was a representation of man prior to sin. The relationship between Adam and God before Adam's sin was ideal. There was absolute clarity and no room for *avodah zarah, idol worship*. Therefore, there was no problem having the graven images of the *kruvim* in the Holy of Holies.

Similarly, the last verse of the second chapter of *Bereishis*, prior to the sin of eating from the *eitz ha'da'as* reads, "*Va'yiyu shneihem arumim ha-adam ve'ishto ve'lo yisboshashu.*"[137] Prior to the sin, Adam and Eve were naked and they felt no shame. In other words, before the concept of sin was actualized in this world there existed a state of absolute purity. Similarly, in the "extraterritorial" Holy of Holies there was absolute purity and holiness. There were, consequently, no concerns of immorality or immodesty in that location.

This fascinating approach of Rav Kook can help explain a difficult part of our *parsha*. Among the seven *mitzvos* contained in *Parshas Tetzaveh*, there is the mitzvah of the *bigdei kehunah*, the specific four garments which a regular *kohein* had to wear, and the four additional pieces, totaling eight garments, which the *kohein gadol* had to don. What is unique about the *bigdei kehunah* is that they contained *shatnez*, wool and linen. The *avneit* (belt) of a regular *kohein*, in particular, as well as the *efod* and *choshen* of the *kohein gadol* contained *shatnez*. The question is, why?

Let us extend Rav Kook's approach. The *Tanchuma* asks why we are not to wear *shatnez*. The Torah does not give a reason for this

---

136 *Oros haMitzvos*, as part of *Otzros haRe'ah chelek 4.*
137 *Bereishis* 2:25.

prohibition. However, in order to understand the mitzvah as best we can, we can look at where we find wool and linen mentioned in the Torah for the first time, which teaches about their essences.

In the story of Kayin and Hevel,[138] Kayin brings an offering of linen. Rashi, on the spot, explains that Kayin brought from that which was of inferior quality. Hevel, on the other hand, brings wool, which the Torah itself testifies was of the best quality ("*mi'bechoros tzono u'mei'chelveihen*"[139]). Hevel was the *tzaddik* and Kayin was not. We see, therefore, that one material, namely the wool of Hevel, represents good and the other, namely the linen of Kayin, represents bad.

Every Friday night, when we sing *Eishes Chayil* in praise of the Jewish woman, we include the praise "*darsha tzemer u'fishtim*,"[140] literally meaning she looks for wool and linen. What is the essence of this praise? Avraham praised his wife, Sarah, for her ability to distinguish between *tzemer* and *pishtim*, good and bad, between Yitzchak and Yishmael, as she sent Yishmael away. We therefore praise the Jewish woman for her values and for her keen sense of being able to distinguish between good and bad.

It is only after the sin that there was this fusion of good and bad, *eitz ha'da'as tov ve'ra*.[141] Prior to the sin, there was a clear demarcation. By extension, the extraterritorial Beis Hamikdash, where the *kohanim* worked, had a clear sense of right and wrong. The *kohanim* could wear *shatnez* because their *avodah* went back to the time prior to Kayin and Hevel.

Interestingly, King Shlomo had on the walls of his *heichal* depictions of the *kruvim*, a male and female in an embracing position. This is because, as we have already mentioned, there was this absolute clarity and absolute purity which existed in the Beis Hamikdash similar to the state in Gan Eden.

The Beis Hamikdash is meant to inspire us in terms of the kind

---

138 *Bereishis* 4.
139 *Bereishis* 4:4.
140 *Mishlei* 31:13.
141 *Bereishis* 2:17.

of homes we build for ourselves. While there is a great deal of confusion, immorality and distraction outside on the street, nevertheless in each and every home, which is to become a *mikdash*, we are to strive for a higher life. The *kohein*, who wore *shatnez* in the Beis Hamikdash, should thereby serve as an example for us that we, too, are to strive to bring absolute clarity and purity into our homes.

May this very fascinating lesson of inspiration of the *mikdash* serve as an elevation for each of our respective homes.

KI SISA
A TASTE OF PARADISE

There is a familiar passage in *Parshas Ki Sisa* which is incorporated as part of the text of the Shabbos morning *Shmoneh Esreh* in *Shacharis*. It is the verse of *"Ve'shamru Vnei Yisrael es haShabbos."*[142] For many people, this passage is included as well as part of the *Kiddush Rabbah*, the Shabbos day *kiddush*.

The question is: What is the Torah adding by saying *"Ve'shamru Vnei Yisrael es haShabbos la'asos es haShabbos le'dorosam bris olam,"*[143] literally, that the Jewish people shall observe the Shabbos to make the Shabbos an eternal covenant for the generations? We were already commanded at Sinai, *"Shamor es yom haShabbos le'kadsho,"*[144] to observe the Shabbos to make it holy! What is added in our *parsha*?

The *Ohr Hachaim Hakadosh* points out that the term *ve'shamru*, literally meaning to guard and to watch, in fact, has additional explanations.

---

142 *Shemos* 31:16.
143 Ibid.
144 *Devarim* 5:12.

He refers us to *Parshas Vayeshev*, where the Torah allows us to listen in to the dreams of Yosef as he shares them with his brothers. Regarding the second dream, in which the sun, the moon and eleven stars all bow down to Yosef, the Torah describes the response of Yaakov as follows. *"Va'yig'ar bo aviv va'yomer lo mah ha'chalom ha'zeh asher chalamta havo navo ani ve'imcha ve'achecha li'hishtachavos lecha artzah."*[145] This literally means that his father [Yaakov] was not very happy, and he scolded him [Yosef] saying, "What is this dream which you have dreamt? Do you really think that I and your mother and your brothers are going to come and bow down to you?"

The Torah continues to describe the response to Yosef's dream. *"Va'yikan'u bo echav ve'aviv shamar es ha'davar,"*[146] his brothers were jealous of him but his father *shamar* — kept the matter in mind. Rashi comments that this means that Yaakov was waiting and yearning for the fulfillment of these dreams.

We can similarly understand our verse in *Parshas Ki Sisa.*

"Ve'shamru Vnei Yisrael es haShabbos" means that the Jewish people are to yearn for and anticipate the Shabbos. One is not to look upon Shabbos as a burden with restrictions as to what one cannot do. Rather, one is to recognize the incredible opportunity and privilege which Shabbos affords us. *"Ve'aviv shamar,"* Yaakov was anticipating, and we too are to yearn and pine for the Shabbos.

This is the first aspect of *Ve'shamru Vnei Yisrael es haShabbos.* The Jewish people are to yearn for Shabbos.

The *Ohr Hachaim Hakadosh* continues and says that Shabbos, as we know, is something sanctified by God. What does it then mean *"la'asos es haShabbos,"*[147] for us to make the Shabbos? After all, Shabbos is something already sanctified! He explains that we have the responsibility of adding on to the Shabbos, as the *gemara* in *Yoma*[148] teaches, *"Le'hosif mei'chol al ha-kodesh."* We are to, literally, take in the Shabbos early and take it out late. This shows our excitement

---

145 *Bereishis* 37:10.
146 Ibid., 37:11.
147 *Shemos* 31:16.
148 81.

and anticipation. Furthermore, that which we add on to Shabbos is *our* contribution to Shabbos. This is *our* making of Shabbos. It fits in with the idea, once again, that we are excited for its coming.

The *gemara* in *Brachos*[149] teaches that Shabbos is one-sixtieth of the World to Come, as we say in our *zemiros*, *"mei'ein Olam Haba,"* that Shabbos is literally a part of the World to Come. It must be, therefore, that Shabbos is more than a day of relaxation. This is not how we anticipate the World to Come!

What is the World to Come? The World to Come is that world in which man is going to appreciate spirituality. His soul is going to be able to connect with God in a way in which it cannot connect in this world. On Shabbos, which is *mei'ein Olam Haba*, says the *Ibn Ezra*, one has the opportunity to partake of the *ruchnius*, some of the spirituality, which one cannot attain during the week.

There is a challenging but exciting *gemara* found at the end of *Kesubos.*[150] We are told that after his passing, Rebbe would literally return to his home, and, explains the *Gilyon Hashas*, recite *kiddush* for the members of his household. One Friday evening, the *gemara* continues, a neighbor came and called at the door. Rebbe's maid-servant said to her, "Shh! Quiet, for Rebbe is sitting within." When Rebbe heard that his visits were now becoming public knowledge, he would no longer come. Why not? He did not want to cause disparagement of other *tzaddikim* who had passed on, as if to say that he was better than them.

Rav Pam, *zt"l,* points out[151] something very special about this *gemara.* We can only imagine the very special share of the World to Come which Rebbe was privileged to enjoy. He did so much for the Jewish people. He was the *Gadol Hador.* He edited the *Mishnah*, which is the mainstay of our Torah study until this very day. He headed the Jewish community politically at a very difficult time. One could therefore only imagine the very special share which Rebbe enjoyed in the World to Come. And yet, he was willing to concede

---

149 57b.
150 103a.
151 Rav Pam *Atara L'melech* p.7.

this portion in order to come back to this world at the occasion of the sanctification of Shabbos at the time of *kiddush*. Wow!

This story in the *gemara Kesubos* demonstrates so poignantly the message in the *gemara Brachos*. When the *gemara* says in *Brachos* that Shabbos is *mei'ein Olam Haba*, a part of the World to Come, it is not simply an expression. It means that we literally have the capacity to bring, as the *brachah* says, "*ve'chayei olam nata be'socheinu,*" part of the eternal world which God plants literally in our midst.

This does not happen by itself. It does not happen merely by abstaining from *melachah*, though this is a necessary prerequisite. This is where it starts. However, after this foundation one has to work at creating a Shabbos table environment. There are numerous ways this may be accomplished. One may choose to follow the model of the Sh"la Hakadosh, who would only speak *lashon ha-kodesh*, i.e., Hebrew, at his Shabbos table. One can make sure that not only is the food served at the Shabbos meal delicious, but that the *divrei Torah* which accompany the food are delicious as well. One can also try to include different *nigunim* for the *zemiros* which are sung at the Shabbos table in order to make them exciting. In any case, whatever one chooses to do in order to enhance the spirit of Shabbos at his meal, the most important thing he can do is to open his Shabbos table to those people who do not yet have the very special gift of Shabbos.

May each one of these enhancements to our Shabbos table help us to attain that very special taste of *Olam Haba* in this world.

VAYAKHEL
MIND OVER MATTER

In describing the construction of the *Mishkan* in the desert, the verse says, *"Va'yavo'u kol ish asher nesa'o libo,"*[152] literally, every man whose heart inspired him came. These are the individuals who came to implement the orders of constructing the sanctuary and all its accoutrements, in the incredible detail which was being asked for by Hashem.

What is this concept of *nesa'o libo*, of an individual who was inspired? The Ramban explains that none of the individuals who worked on the construction of the sanctuary were specially educated in this field of labor. They did not attend architectural schools or engineering schools. How then were they to perform the incredible craftsmanship required?

The answer is that these individuals had one thing going for them, namely *nesa'o libo*, their heart inspired them. They had what is known in Hebrew as *yuzmah*, which means not simply enthusiasm but conviction, persistence and dedication. Because they wanted to be an active part of the construction of this sanctuary with such an incredible desire, God enabled them to so do.

---

152 *Shemos* 35:21.

We have all heard stories from the Holocaust that the Nazis, *yemach shmam* (may their names be erased), would announce, "Anyone here a tailor?" People hoped that maybe their need for someone who was skilled might save them. People, therefore, volunteered and said, "Yes, I'm a tailor." In reality, however, they had never threaded a needle in their lives, let alone made one single stitch in a garment. What happened? Overnight, they became tailors — and good ones, at that — because their lives depended on it.

Here too, in regard to constructing the *Mishkan*, the volunteers realized how important their mission was. Because of their conviction, God subsequently responded in kind and gave them the ability to implement that which they so desired.

This concept of *yuzmah* is found in a very fascinating *midrash* in *Devarim Rabbah*. The wise King Solomon says in *Mishlei*, "*Lech el nemala atzel*"[153] — You lazy one, go to the ant; you are to learn a certain way of life from that little species, the ant.

It is amazing that 2,000 years ago our Rabbis had such a sophisticated knowledge of science and nature. The Rabbis tells us the following. The average life expectancy of an ant is six months. How much food does he need for his entire lifetime? A *chitah u'mechtzah*, one kernel of wheat and a half. This is all he needs to get by his six months of existence. What does the ant subsequently do? He busies himself all summer long gathering much more than that mere *chitah u'mechtzah*. Why? He reasons that perhaps God will grant him longevity. The ant says, "I will outlive my father and my grandfather and my *alte zeide* the ant, all of whom lived only for six months. And should I be blessed with longevity, I will have what to eat." Wow! Rather than take the easy way out and say, "I already have my *chitah u'mechtzah*, I already have what I need and now I can relax and take it easy," the ant is not lazy. In fact, just the opposite, he is busy and working all the time trying to improve his situation.

Most people are not satisfied if they accomplish this year what they did last year. The goal is to always do better and do more. While

---

153 *Mishlei* 6:6.

this is true in the realm of materialism, it has to be true, as well, in the realm of spirituality. A person cannot be satisfied with the way he is now. He must strive to be better.

The *navi Yeshaya* speaks about individuals whose lives are focused in "*mitzvas anashim melumada*,"[154] meaning that they perform their *mitzvos* in a rote manner. It is a habit. They did it this way last year. They did it this way the year before. The Radak, in his commentary on this verse, notes how tragic it is that individuals are not growing. They have no *yuzmah*. They have no *she'ifah*, burning desire. Unfortunately, there is no such thing as standing still. If you do not go up, you are heading in the other direction.

It is for this reason that the Torah suggests, "*Ve'lo sa'ale be'ma'alos al mizbechi*,"[155] you are not to go up by steps to My altar. There is not to be a staircase leading up to the altar. The *kohein* had to go up on a ramp. Why?

I heard a very powerful insight into this question from one of my teachers, the late Rav Besden, *zt"l*. He notes the difference between a staircase and a ramp. On a staircase, a person can walk a few steps and pause. Someone with a heart condition can walk up the steps slowly and catch his breath. It is much more challenging to stop on a ramp. One either goes up or down.

Each of us has to search deep within our hearts and find that great spark of *nesa'o libo* with which God has endowed each and every one of us.

---

154 *Yeshaya* 29:13.
155 *Shemos* 20:23.

PEKUDEI
ACCOUNTABILITY

The word *pekudei* literally means an accounting. In *Parshas Pekudei*, Moshe does just that. He gives an accounting of how the various precious items which were donated, were dispersed and used on behalf of the *Mishkan*.

Why does he do this? After all, the Torah testifies in *Parshas Beha'alosecha* that God Himself says regarding Moshe, "*Be'chol beisi ne'eman hu*,"[156] he is the most trustworthy in My entire household. God trusts Moshe. So, why then is he of all people required to give an accounting?

The *midrash* in *Shemos Rabbah*[157] addresses this difficulty. The verse in *Parshas Ki Sisa* reads, "*Ve'hibitu acharei Moshe*,"[158] the people would peer after Moshe. There were those who would stare at him and say, "Look how fortunate Moshe is that he has a direct line to God." Others would say, "Look at Moshe, he has access to all the gold and silver collected on behalf of the *Mishkan*; it can't be that he did

---

not line some of his pockets with some of the goods." As soon as Moshe hears this comment, he says, "I have to give an accounting."

Moshe thus teaches us that there is an added responsibility to fulfill. We need to regularly "give an accounting" of our lives — to ourselves and to God. Are we acting correctly? Are we learning as much Torah as we can? Are we keeping the *mitzvos* properly? This is an important process, but it is not enough. The verse says, "*Ve'hiyisem neki'im mei'Hashem u'mi'Yisrael*,"[159] and you shall be free of guilt from before Hashem and before Israel. It is important for a person to be beyond suspicion. A person should be clearly respected not only by God, Who knows what he is doing is correct. He should also be clearly respected by man. One has to avoid what is *halachically* termed *maris ayin*, looking suspicious.

It is for this reason, interestingly, that the Rabbis teach us the following *mishnah* in *Shkalim*.[160] When they withdrew the monies, i.e., the *machatzis ha-shekel* (the half-shekel coins which were given by every Jewish male over the age of twenty), in order to purchase new sacrifices, we are told that the person who went in to take the money out could not wear a hemmed garment, such as one with a cuff, on his pants. He could not wear shoes or sandals either. He could not wear *tefillin* or an amulet as he went in to get the money. The reason for these restrictions is because perhaps this person will become poor and the people will say that the reason he became poor is because he took from the *Mishkan*. It is also possible that this person may become rich and the people will say that he became rich off the donations to the *Mishkan*.

The *gemara* in *Yoma*[161] gives examples of families of *kehunah* (priestly families), who were involved in the daily operations of the Beis Hamikdash. For example, the *gemara* tells us of the family of Garmu who was involved in the *lechem ha-panim* — they made the showbread. The *gemara* relates that refined bread was never found in the hands of their children. The reason for this was that people should not say that they are being fed from the *lechem ha-panim*.

---

159 *Bamidbar* 32:22, concerning Bnai Gad and Reuven.
160 3:2.
161 38a.

Another priestly family, Avtinas, were specialists in the preparation of the *ketores*, the incense. We are told that never did a bride go out of their house with perfume on. Moreover, even when a girl from outside their family married into their family the condition was, "No perfume." This was done so that people should not say that they are leaving over some of the *ketores* for their own benefit!

A different *gemara* in *Yoma*[162] tells us of the tremendous responsibility which we each have for one other. Each Jew is to be a role model for the other. On the one hand, I have a responsibility that when I see someone doing something which appears to me to be wrong I have to say to myself, "*Hevei dan es kol ha'adam le'chaf zechus*,"[163] I have to find a way of judging him favorably. He, on the other hand, cannot put himself in a situation which is one of *maris ayin*, which does not appear exactly right in the eyes of man.

Rav Moshe Feinstein, *zt"l* was known to say that each individual is to view himself as a *mishkan* (sanctuary). One may ask, "Why does it make a difference how I live my life? Of what significance is it?" The answer is that you are literally the *merkavah* (chariot) for the *Shechinah* (God's Presence). It is therefore not about you. It is about what you represent. It is about the *Shechinah*. It is about God. People look at you. They looked at Moshe and saw the *Shechinah*. They said, "Moshe, the man of God, may have taken from the donations to the *Mishkan* and he may have put it in his pockets." God, of course, knew that this was not true. Moshe nevertheless had to defend the honor and the glory of God in the eyes of the people by taking an accounting, because each Jew is representative of God.

The *parsha* is communicating to each and every Jew how important he or she is. It is too dangerous for us to rely upon "*hevei dan es kol ha'adam le'chaf zechus*," because maybe the fellow will not judge you favorably. After all, you represent nothing but the *Shechinah*.

What a very special way to end the Book of Redemption!

---

162 86.
163 *Pirkei Avos* 1:6.

VAYIKRA
DERECH ERETZ KADMA LA'TORAH

The opening verse of *Sefer Vayikra* reads: "*Va'yikra el Moshe va'yidaber Hashem eilav,*"[164] God calls to Moshe and speaks to him from the *Ohel Mo'ed* (Tent of Meeting). Our Rabbis[165] note that the first three words, "*Va'yikra el Moshe,*" seem to be extraneous. The Torah could have simply said, as it often does, "And God said to Moshe, saying." What message is being imparted to us by the Torah's use of the word *va'yikra,* that God called him?

Our Rabbis derive from this verse[166] that any Torah scholar who does not have good character is worse than a dead carcass. Go and learn from Moshe Rabbeinu, says the *midrash*. Moshe is literally the father of wisdom and the father of the prophets. He led us out of Egypt. Through him, many miracles happened in Egypt, not to mention the wonders at the sea. Moshe ascended to the heavens and

---

164 *Vayikra* 1:1.
165 *Vayikra Rabbah* 1:15.
166 Ibid.

subsequently brought down the Torah. And yet, with all this, Moshe does not go into the sanctuary *until* God summons him, and he is thereby invited to enter. The proof for this is the opening verse of the Book of *Vayikra*, "*Va'yikra el Moshe vayidaber Hashem eilav*," God first calls to Moshe and invites him to come into the Tent of Meeting, and then He proceeds to speak to him.

According to the Ramban[167], the *Mishkan* was the continuity of Sinai. Just as God began the process of giving the Torah at Sinai, He thereby continued this process in the *Mishkan*. The *Mishkan* was set up for the Torah, yet there is one step which precedes entry into the *Mishkan*. "*Derech eretz kadma la'Torah*," good character, *menschlichkeit*, is a prerequisite for Torah.

Thus, the first three words of *Sefer Vayikra* teach that Moshe displays a characteristic lack of arrogance. One perhaps could have imagined that now that the *Mishkan* was ready, Moshe would simply walk right in. After all, that is the purpose of the *Mishkan*. The *midrash* is teaching us, though, that a *talmid chacham* must have good *middos*, one example of which means waiting to be invited before entering.

This attitude of humility and *derech eretz* is in contrast to the *neveilah*, the dead carcass. What is a *neveilah*? By definition, a *neveilah* is a kosher animal which never made it to the finish line, meaning it never underwent *shechitah*, ritual slaughter. This animal had great potential. It could have fed many hungry families. When we had a Beis Hamikdash, it could have been used as a *korban* (sacrifice). Now, however, what is the best one can do with it? He can sell it to a non-Jew.

A *talmid chacham* has great potential. However, if the *talmid chacham* has not integrated the Torah which he has learned as a fundamental part of his personality, then his worth is even less than that of a *neveilah*. He may very well have the potential, demonstrated by his vast knowledge. If, however, his Torah knowledge has not become an integral part of his character, it does not reflect well on him or the Torah. In fact, it is even worse than a *neveilah* — because

---

167   *Ramban Shemos* 25:2.

there is absolutely no use for that person whatsoever. What a powerful *midrash* this is!

Based upon the verse, "*Hoi kol tzamei lechu la'mayim,*"[168] everyone who is thirsty go to the water, the *gemara* in *Taanis*[169] teaches that the thirst one has for Torah is likened to the thirst one has for water. What is the connection between Torah and water? Rebbe Chanina bar Idi taught that just as water leaves a high level and goes to a lower level, so too the words of Torah are only perpetuated and retained by one who is humble. Humility is the *derech eretz*, which is *kadma la'Torah*. Humility is a prerequisite for Torah.

In the *sefer Hama'or she'ba'Torah,*[170] Rav Sholom Zvi haKohen Shapiro, zt"l comments on the verse at the end of *Parshas Mishpatim*, "*Ve'nigash Moshe levado,*"[171] Moshe alone went up to *Shamayim* to receive the Torah. Where were the *zekeinim*, the elders, who accompanied Moshe to the mountain? They were not allowed to ascend, and complained about it. God thereby explained to them that this was *middah ke'neged middah*, measure for measure. "In Egypt, when you were gathered by Moshe to accompany him as he went to speak with Pharoah, you were scared and dropped out along the way. As a result, Moshe and Aharon went in alone." Since they didn't join Moshe at the time of difficulty, they weren't allowed to join him at the time of exultation.

What about Aharon? Aharon *did* accompany Moshe when they went to Pharoah! Why didn't he join Moshe up to *Shamayim* to receive the Torah?

The *Midrash Hagadol* explains that Aharon stayed behind in order not to embarrass the *zekeinim*. Imagine! Aharon forgoes his own personal growth and his own ability to go up to *Shamayim* in order not to make them feel bad. This is what it means to have *derech eretz*. It includes being sensitive towards the next one — the way you conduct yourself in a store, the way you wait your turn in line, the man-

---

168 *Yeshaya* 55:1.
169 7a.
170 As brought down by Reb Baruch Simon in his introduction to *Sefer Shemos*.
171 *Shemos* 24:2.

ner in which you present yourself to people, and so much more.

There is a beautiful story told about the Chazon Ish, who used to dance on Simchas Torah to the point that he was so tired that two *talmidim* had to walk him home. He literally would not have been able to stand on his own without their assistance.

As he was walking home one Simchas *Torah*, he said *Gut Yontef* to a certain Jew. The Jew said, "Rebbe, what kind of a *gut yontef* is it? To me, it's not a *gut yontef*. I'm new in this community and no one has said *Gut Yontef* to me. No one has welcomed me. I haven't been made to feel welcome in any *shul*, with any *hakafos*." As soon as he heard this, the Chazon Ish asked the Jew what his favorite *niggun* was. Whatever it was, the Chazon Ish immediately started to dance before this Jew in the street together with the two *talmidim* in the same way he would dance before a *chasan*. He did this not merely for a minute or two, but, as exhausted as he was, he did it for ten, fifteen minutes.

This true story exemplifies *derech eretz kadma la'Torah*. To make another Jew feel good on Simchas Torah comes before a person's own individual *simchah* of Torah.

During the period of the second Beis Hamikdash, there was Torah and there was the observance of *mitzvos*. So why the *churban*? Without *middos tovos*, good character, there is no Torah.

As we prepare for Pesach, our job is not simply to look for Cheerios which may have rolled under the refrigerator. Rather, *derech eretz kadma la'Torah*.

Our job is to internalize the lesson imparted to us by the first three words of *Sefer Vayikra, Va'yikra el Moshe*. In order to truly receive the Torah and live the Torah, we must improve our character in a fitting manner.

TZAV
IS GOD IN OUR MIDST?

During a leap year in the Jewish calendar, when an additional month of Adar is added, we read *Parshas Tzav* in conjunction with Purim. Let us try and understand the connection between the *parsha* and Purim.

In the *gemara* in *Yoma*,[172] Rav Asi explains that the twenty-second chapter of *Tehillim*, which begins "*La'menatzei'ach al ayeles ha'shachar,*" is a prophecy which King David said regarding Esther. *Ayeles ha'shachar* literally refers to the dawn. Rav Asi explains that just as the morning is the end of the entire night, so too Esther represents the end of all the miracles.

This is a rather challenging piece of *gemara*. One of my teachers shared a thought-provoking insight. When Rav Asi tells us that Esther is the end of all the miracles, is it a positive statement or a negative one?

In order to understand this, consider Amalek's battle with *Bnei Yisrael*.[173] Before Amalek arrived, in the paragraph before, the Torah

---

172   29a.
173   *Shemos* 17:18.

tells us that the Jewish people were in the desert. They lacked water, and so they complained to Moshe. "What did you do? How could you bring us here?" God instructs Moshe to hit the rock.[174] Moshe complies, and water comes out. They consequently name the place Masa U'Meriva,[175] because it is where they tested God saying, *"Ha'yesh Hashem be'kirbeinu im ayin"* — Is God in our midst or not?[176]

Immediately following this verse, *"Va'yavo Amalek,"*[177] Amalek attacks.

The Netziv, in his commentary, is troubled. What kind of question is this? How could a people who had experienced the plagues in Egypt and had personally witnessed the splitting of the Red Sea, possibly ask "Is God in our midst or not?"

The Netziv explains: There is no question that at this moment *Bnei Yisrael* knew that God was in their midst. They reasoned, however, that this was only now because they have a leader such as Moshe Rabbeinu who had such a close connection with God. What, though, would be in the future? Really, they were asking, "Will God be in our midst in the future?" Due to the Jews' lack of faith, Amalek, the symbol of happenstance, comes. If you doubt God, what happens? Amalek comes.

Until the end of the first Beis Hamikdash, it was clear that God was in the Jewish people's midst. *Yesh Hashem be'kirbeinu.* There were overt and open miracles in the Beis Hamikdash.[178] During the period of seventy years following the destruction of the first Beis Hamikdash, the Jewish people had doubts. Therefore, Haman, a descendant of Amalek, comes along.

The Purim story showed us in a most definitive way that *yesh Hashem be'kirbeinu*, God is indeed with us. He does not need to be with us in an obviously supernatural way. Rather, God arranges the

---

174 This was in the first year, in contrast to the fortieth year when He instructed Moshe to speak to the rock.
175 Ibid., 17:7.
176 Ibid.
177 Ibid., 17:8.
178 See *Pirkei Avos* 5:7.

natural order of things. When you read through the Book of Esther, from chapter one through chapter ten, each step along the way, you do not see any miracles. In the beginning of the Purim story, a king gets drunk and orders his queen to come. This is not supernatural. Next in the story, he has her killed and he wants another queen in her stead. This is nothing beyond the norm either. When Mordechai understands and discovers the plot of Bigsan and Seresh, there is nothing special about this as well. You can move from page to page in the *megillah*, and everything happens in a natural way. Yet, what is the *brachah* we recite upon reading the *megillah*? *She'asa nisim la'avoseinu*, God performed miracles for our ancestors. As a result of the Purim story, the Jewish people realized that God is with them in the everyday natural course of events.

We can now revisit the *gemara* in *Yoma*, with which we began. *Megillas Esther* is full of hidden *nisim* (miracles) because, explains the *Yaaras Devash*, Reb Yonasan Eibeschitz, we do not need open miracles anymore. As a result of Purim, we recognize God in the everyday. Therefore, one very important lesson of Purim is for each and every one of us to bolster our faith in God and to recognize that God is with us, even though He is usually hidden.

This indeed is a very clear tie-in to *Parshas Tzav*. One of the *mitzvos* in *Parshas Tzav* is the *korban todah*, the thanksgiving sacrifice. There are four categories of situations for which a person is required to bring a *korban todah*.[179] For example, if a person was very sick and now has been healed, or he was in a dangerous situation, such as having crossed the sea or traveled through a desert. By bringing a thanksgiving offering,[180] he is saying that it is not by chance that he is cured or saved from danger; it is an affirmation of *yesh Hashem be'kirbeinu*.

May the *zechus*, the merit, of the *emunah* and the *bitachon* which come out of the Purim story serve us in good stead for the great events which are, please God, forthcoming.

---

179 See *Brachos* 54b.

180 Today, in the absence of the *korban todah*, anyone who finds himself or herself saved from a dangerous situation recites the *brachah* known as "*haGomel.*"

SHMINI
FOOD FOR THE SOUL

A ccording to the *Sefer haChinuch*, *Parshas Shmini* contains seventeen *mitzvos*. Of these, the last thirteen *mitzvos* focus on the laws of *kashrus*, the dietary laws of the Jewish people.

Interestingly, the *Sefer haChinuch* writes[181] as follows:

> At the root of this precept, namely *kashrus*, lies the basic concept that the body is an instrument of the spirit. With the body, the spirit carries out its activity. Without the body, the spirit can never complete its work. The spirit thereby comes into the shadow of the body only for the benefit of the spirit and not for its harm. For God never does harm. Rather, He does only good for all of His creations. Thus, we find that the body at the command of the spirit is to be

---

181 Regarding Mitzvah 73, in *Parshas Mishpatim*, where the Torah teaches us not to eat the meat from an animal which is *treifah*, torn by beasts (*Shemos* 22:30).

compared to a pair of tongs in the hand of a blacksmith or any other toolmaker. With the tongs, the craftsman can produce a tool fit for its intended purpose. Now, in truth, if the tongs are strong and properly shaped in such manner that one is able to grasp tools in them, the craftsman can make tools efficiently. If the tongs are not good, the tools will never come out properly shaped and fit.

Similarly, if there is loss or damage of any kind in and to the body, some function of intelligence will be nullified corresponding to that defect. For this reason, our complete and perfect Torah has removed us far from anything which causes such defect. It is in this vein, according to the plain meaning, we can say that we were given a ban by the Torah against all forbidden foods. If there are among any of these foods those whose harm is known and understood neither by us nor by the wise men of medicine, do not wonder about them. The faithful, trustworthy Physician, who adjured us about them, is wiser than both you and them. How foolish and hasty would anyone be who thought that nothing is harmful or useful, except as He understands it.

In simple English, the *Chinuch* is saying that the Torah (via the laws of *kashrus*) is providing us with a means of fortifying and protecting the precious soul which is within our body.

Indeed, the *gemara*[182] points to a verse in our *parsha* where the Torah speaks about the negative effect upon our bodies of eating the forbidden foods. The Torah uses the phrase *"ve'nitmeisem bam,"*[183]

---

182 *Yoma* 39b.
183 *Vayikra* 11:43.

which means that you shall become defiled through them. That is the *way it is read*. The *way it is written*, however, is missing an *aleph*. In other words, it is written *u'netamtem*, you will become dull-hearted. This means that you will lose your sensitivity to a higher quality and perspective of life. The physical act of eating affects our spiritual sensitivities.

Indeed, our people have maintained an incredible spiritual sensitivity throughout the millennia. This sensitivity stems from none other than our loyalty to Torah; central to it are the laws of *kashrus*.

There was a special *yehi ratzon*, a special prayer, which the Jews in the concentration camp in Buchenwald recited before they ate *chametz* on Pesach. This prayer was distributed to them by the Rabbis with the following preface. "Before you eat the *chametz*, you should say *be'kavanas ha'lev*, with the full intent of the heart:"

אבינו שבשמים, הנה גלוי וידוע לפניך שרצוננו
לעשות רצונך, לחגוג את חג הפסח באכילת מצה
ובשמירת איסור חמץ. אך על זאת דאב ליבנו,
שהשעבוד מעכב אותנו, ואנחנו שרויים בסכנת
נפשות. הננו מוכנים ומזומנים לקיים מצוותך
'וחי בהם׳ [במצוות], ולא שימות בהם ולהיזהר
באזהרתך 'הישמר לך ושמור נפשך מאוד'. כן,
על תפילתנו לך, שתתחיינו ותקיימנו ותגאלנו במהרה
לשמור חוקיך ולעשות רצונך ולעבדך בלבב שלם -
אמן.

Father in Heaven, it is known before You that it is our desire to do Your will and to celebrate and to observe the Festival of Passover by eating matzah and by desisting and refraining from eating *chametz*. For this our hearts are pained that the servitude in which we find ourselves, prevents us and we find ourselves literally in the peril of, God forbid, losing our lives. We are therefore prepared to fulfill Your commandment, where the Torah teaches in *Parshas Acharei Mos*, "*va'chai bahem*,"[184] you are to live the laws of Torah, *ve'lo she'yamus bahem*, and not that the laws of Torah should be an instrument which causes our death. We will further be careful with that which You have taught us "*hishamer lecha u'shmor nafshecha me'od*,"[185] that we have an obligation to protect our bodies. Therefore, our prayer is the *she'hecheyanu ve'kiamanu*, which we were privileged to recite on the night on Pesach, that You should sustain us and maintain our existence. We pray that You shall redeem us quickly so that we will have the opportunity to guard and to observe Your statutes and to do Your will and to serve You with completeness of heart. Amen.

This is how they ate *chametz* in Buchenwald.

Moshe Perl, a survivor of Radom, wrote the following story:[186]

In 1945, in the labor camp Feidingun we suffered greatly from frost and starvation on the one hand and from typhus on the other. Many died due to disease and others from the blows of the SS guards, *yemach shemam*. And still a group in this environment, as Pesach was approaching, was concerned how to abstain from eating *chametz*. I was afraid of *chametz* more than I feared death itself, which was present constantly.

---

184 *Vayikra* 18:5.
185 *Devarim* 4:9.
186 From the Hebrew, in "*Be'kedushah U'be'gvurah*" by Yehoshua Eibeschutz.

Several days before Pesach, an SS officer walked into the factory where I was working as a sign maker. He approached me about designing models and targets for target practice for the SS soldiers, which could be reused, the holes filled in again.

In a flash, an idea came to me which I presented to the SS officer. A large target with the form of a soldier, wearing a helmet, should be the picture, which will serve as the target. "However," I said to the officer, "to accomplish your unusual request to refill the holes I need a great deal of flour in order to make a great deal of glue which can be used to plug the holes." On the spot, the SS officer issued a written order for five kilo of flour. I saw in this the "*etzba Elokim*,"[187] literally, the finger of God.

When I approached the one in charge of the pantry and presented the authorization for flour, and when I explained why, he smiled and said, "I suspect you will use some for the baking of matzah for Passover." He told me that he recalled the special taste of matzah, which he had eaten by a Czech Jew several years ago. At first, I was astonished that he unveiled the true intent of my heart. However, I restated and retorted immediately to him, "If you will give me an additional five kilo, I'll bake matzah for you." "You've got a deal," he responded, and a new bag of flour was opened. My brother, Meir, and the others witnessed this open miracle. Our joy was indescribable.

---

187   See *Shemos* 8:15; *Yoma* 39b; *Vayikra* 11:43; Ibid., 18:5; *Devarim* 4:9; From the Hebrew, in "*Be'kedushah U'be'gvurah*" by Yehoshua Eibeschutz; See *Shemos* 8:15.

Together, we pooled our resources. A carpenter from Radom made a *nudelholtz*, a rolling pin. We found something to make the holes, glass shards we used to shave down logs of wood on which we prepared the dough. On a thrown-out remnant of an oven, we improvised by gathering several bricks. In almost total darkness behind closed doors and windows, we, Sholom Ciberkayin, Yaakov Leventhal, Gavriel Bergman, Hershel London, my brother Meir, myself, and several other Jews baked matzahs.

In the middle, the *kapo*, Yechiel Friedman, came in. We were filled with fright and terror. When he saw what we were doing, he told us to lower the flame as the smoke was somewhat visible outside and it could endanger us all. All he asked for was a matzah for himself.

Finally, where to hide the matzah? We hid them under the rafters of the roof. The word quickly spread. And just our baking of the matzah ignited in many the spirit and sparks of the Jew, which is present within his identity.

One last story: A certain Rav Ehrenberg, *zt"l,* was a *rav* in Hungary before the war. He survived the war and came to Eretz Yisrael, where he became a *rav* in Petach Tikva. During the war, unfortunately, when the Nazis, *yemach shemam,* were shooting Jews and were burying them in a mass grave, he and others had the terrible job of filling in the earth. When he saw that one Jew was still moving, he stopped. When the SS guard approached him and said, "Why are you not working?" He said, "I can't put the dirt on him lest I kill him. He's still alive." So the SS guard said to him, "Do your work or I will shoot you." Rav Ehrenberg opened up his shirt and said, "Shoot." But the SS guard shot the one on the ground instead.

Where does the Jew get this incredible appreciation for life?

The answer is: We are what we eat. Our special Jewish diet is really food for the soul. Thus we can appreciate how *Parshas Shmini* ends, "*Ki ani Hashem ha-ma'ale eschem mei'eretz Mitzrayim*,"[188] for I am Hashem who brings you up from the land of Egypt. Rashi comments that all over the Torah it does not say *ha-ma'ale* but *hotzeisi*, I brought you out. Here, however, it says "*ha-ma'ale*," I bring you up. Why? Because this is *ma'alyusa hi le'gabaihu*. The privilege of our keeping kosher is literally an elevation for the Jewish people.

Let us remember the incredible *mesiras nefesh* of those who literally gave up their lives to maintain the laws of keeping kosher. Doing so is the key to Judaism — and to maintaining and deepening our spiritual sensitivity. How proud we are to pass on this legacy to further generations to give honor to their memory.

---

188 *Vayikra* 11:45.

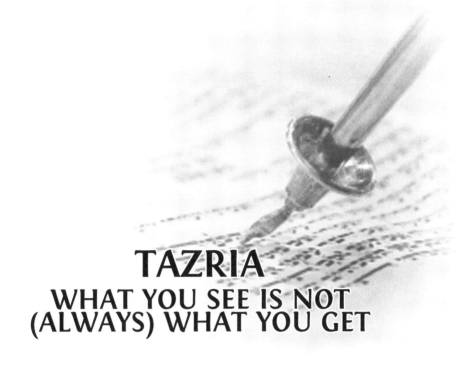

TAZRIA
WHAT YOU SEE IS NOT (ALWAYS) WHAT YOU GET

Most of our *parsha* deals with the laws of *tzara'as*, which is often called leprosy, for lack of a better word. It is certainly not the classic textbook leprosy. The Torah is not a first-aid book. It doesn't tell you what to put on a burn, so the very fact that the Torah speaks about *tzara'as*, the Ramban[189] tells us, indicates its great importance in several ways. First, this phenomenon occurs only in the Land of Israel. Second, it reveals a very special relationship between God and the Jewish people. If and when we veer from the proper course, Hakadosh Baruch Hu immediately intercedes to set us right.

The verse reads: *"Ve'ra'ah hakohein acharei hukabeis es ha'nega ve'hinei lo hafach ha-nega es eino ve'ha-nega lo fasa,"*[190] the *kohein* shall look after the affliction has been washed and behold the affliction has not changed its color and the affliction has not spread. It is interesting to note that the Torah uses the word *eino* here when it is

---

189   *Ramban Vayikra* 13:47.
190   *Vayikra* 13:55.

speaking about the appearance of the *nega* (affliction). Throughout the appearance of the *nega* (the affliction), the term *marei*, appearance, is used. Here, and here alone, the Torah uses the word *eino*, meaning, literally, its eye. Why?

The Ben Ish Chai explains: When an individual may unfortunately be afflicted with all different kinds of *tzaros*, how should he respond? He is to look upon them and realize that he does not understand why they have come, but he knows where they are coming from. He understands that they are coming from a good source. He understands the well-known teaching of Rebbe Akiva that *kol de'avid Rachmana le'tav avid*, as the *gemara* in *Brachos*[191] imparts, all that God does is for the good. Moreover, Rebbe Akiva was a student of Nachum Ish Gamzu about whom the *gemara* in *Taanis*[192] relates that at every incident which occurred to him he was wont to say "*gam zu le'tovah,*" this too is for the good. One is to have a positive attitude — even towards the things that are challenging — and understand that they are, in fact, wholly good.

The Ben Ish Chai takes the verse in *Koheles*,[193] where the wise King Solomon says "*He-chacham einav be'rosho.*" The literal translation of this phrase is that the eyes of the wise man are in his head. A person reading this may say to himself, "For this you have to be the wisest of men?" The Rabbis, therefore, understand this phrase to mean that the outstanding characteristic of the *chacham*, the wise man, is that he contemplates the effects of his actions. In other words, before the *gemara* teaches us, it is Shlomo HaMelech who said it first. "*Eizehu chacham? Ha-ro'eh es ha-nolad.*"[194] Who is the wise man? The one who can see the future consequences of his actions.

The Ben Ish Chai explains what is meant by "*he-chacham einav be'rosho.*" The following interpretation is not the literal understanding, but it nevertheless shows the incredible depth of Torah. The Ben Ish Chai interprets *einav* in this verse to mean his *ayin*, referring to

---

191 60b.
192 21a.
193 2:14.
194 *Tamid* 32a.

the Hebrew letter *ayin*. The verse is thereby translated as follows. The *ayin* of the wise man is at the head. What does this mean? The word *nega* is composed of three Hebrew letters, *nun*, then *gimmel*, then *ayin*. A wise man puts the letter *ayin* at the *rosh*, the beginning. So transpose the letters by taking the letter *ayin*, which is the last letter in the word *nega*, and place it at the beginning of the word. The order of the letters is now *ayin*, *nun*, *gimmel*, or *oneg*, meaning pleasure. *Nega* means affliction, something which is only negative. *Oneg* is the opposite — a delight! Through this creativity, the Ben Ish Chai is able to find and to see the positive, even within the negative.

With this explanation, the Ben Ish Chai understands the second verse of *Parshas Metzora* in a new light. The Torah instructs, *"Ve'ra'ah ha-kohein ve'hinei nirpah nega ha'tzara'as min ha'tzaruah."*[195] The *kohein* will see and behold the affliction has been healed from the person who was afflicted. It appears that the last two words in this verse, *min ha-tzaruah*, from the one who has *tzara'as*, are superfluous. "No," says the Ben Ish Chai, "that is exactly the emphasis of the verse. It comes *min ha'tzaruah*. It comes from the person. It comes from his realization that there is meaning hiding behind everything which God does. It is not leprosy. It is not nature. Realizing this is a very positive kind of attitude, which the Ben Ish Chai is telling us that the Torah is teaching within the *parsha* of *nega'im* (afflictions).

In the *sefer Aleinu Le'shabeiach*, Rav Zilberstein, *shlita* from Eretz Yisrael writes about a patient in Eretz Yisrael who was literally bereft of his eyesight for several years. With medical advances, an ophthalmologist said to him, "I really believe that with surgery you will once again be able to see." One can only imagine the excitement. The doctor, who at the time was a not-yet observant Jew, said to his patient, "Tell me, I'm curious. What is the first thing which you are looking forward to see when you will get your eyesight back?" Now, you and I might have imagined that he would say a sunset, a grandchild, perhaps a TV program. What would anyone say?

Do you know what this Jew said? This amazing Jew said to his

---

195 *Vayikra* 14:3.

doctor, "The first thing I want to see is my *tzitzis*." Why? The Torah says in conjunction with the mitzvah of *tzitzis*, "*U're'isem oso*,"[196] you shall see them. As a result of which, you shall then remember all the *mitzvos* of God. The patient explained, "If God is going to do this favor for me and restore my eyesight, the least I can do is to show my appreciation to Him and see His *mitzvos* and thereby be reminded of the rest of the *mitzvos*." The doctor was very impressed. He said, "If this is what my patient can be so excited about, I have to look into this." And sure enough, the doctor's life was transformed.

Who should be more grateful to God, this Jew or those of us who always had our eyesight?

Current medical research shows that people with an optimistic outlook are more likely to recover from their illnesses. The Ben Ish Chai must be smiling and saying, "We had it first." When the Torah speaks of that *nega* (affliction), the *nega* is unfortunately *be'eino*, meaning that it remains as it is and it has not been transformed. If only we learn the powerful lesson of "*chacham einav be'rosho*," of putting the letter *ayin* not at the end, which represents a depressed, challenging way to God, but at the beginning, which represents just the opposite. By understanding that whatever He does is for the good, we will partake in great *oneg*, a closer personal relationship with Hakadosh Baruch Hu.

---

196 *Bamidbar* 15:39.

METZORA
BEHIND CLOSED DOORS

The *Be'er Yosef*, Rav Yosef Salant, brings two fascinating *gemaras* as part of his discussion of *Parshas Metzora*. The first *gemara* (in *Arachin*[197]) relates a verse from *Tehillim* where King David says, *"Mah yitein lecha u'mah yosif lach lashon remiah,"*[198] what can He give to you and what can He add to you, o' deceitful tongue? Hakadosh Baruch Hu says to the tongue, "All of a person's limbs are upright and you, the tongue, lie prone." In other words, the tongue remains in a passive position. Hashem continues in conversation with the tongue, "All of a person's limbs are external and you, the tongue, are internal." Moreover, says God to the tongue, "I have encompassed you within two walls, one of bone and one of flesh." These two walls are none other than the teeth and the lips. In other words, *mah yitein lecha u'ma yosif lach*, what further safeguard could God add to prevent the tongue from speaking *lashon hara*?! What an insightful idea that God places the tongue behind two walls!

---

197 15b.
198 *Tehillim* 120:3.

The second *gemara* is found in *Brachos*.[199] There, the *gemara* says in the name of Rav Chisda, that when a person enters the *beis ha-knesses* (synagogue) he should always enter through two doors. What does it mean that he is to enter through *no less than* two doors? There are several interpretations of this *gemara*. First, Rashi understands it to mean that when he enters the *shul* he should not sit close to the door. Rather, he should enter and move in the distance of two doors, equivalent to approximately eight *amos*, so as not to give the impression that he is in a rush to leave. This seemingly simple act serves to demonstrate that going to *shul* in order to pray to God within the context of a *minyan* is not a burden on him. He therefore moves further into the *beis ha-knesses*. The Maharam of Rotenberg writes as well that a person should move in as he enters the synagogue so that he is not distracted by that which is going on outside every time the door opens.

The *Rosh* understands this *gemara* to mean that when one walks into the *beis ha-knesses* he should wait the distance and the time it would take to walk that eight *amos*. The idea is that he should not start *davening* immediately as he enters. He should, rather, pause for a few moments to collect his thoughts.

It is the *Bach*, however, who understands this *gemara* most literally. When the *gemara* says that a person should always enter the *beis ha'knesses* through two doors, the *Bach* understands this to mean that the synagogue should be built in such a way that there are structurally two doors through which to enter. Ideally, the structure of every synagogue should be such that when one opens the door from the street there is a vestibule and then he walks into the *beis ha-knesses* through, literally, a second door. The *Bach* gives a very interesting explanation for this idea, which shows the uniqueness of the Judaism. It was prevalent in other cultures that when one came to make a request from the king, he stood outside and an emissary went to speak to the king on his behalf. We, however, as the Jewish people, have the capacity and extraordinary privilege whereby

---

199 8a.

we can go ourselves, with no intermediary, and stand before *Melech Malchei haMelachim* (King of kings) *Hakadosh Baruch Hu*. Therefore, we enter through both doors — in other words, all the way — in order to approach God Himself.

The *Be'er Yosef* adds to this a very sharp insight, of which the Chofetz Chaim, *zt"l,* makes mention as well. When a person comes before God, his primary instrument of communication is his mouth. If he has not abused the tongue by speaking *lashon hara*, then he will be able to pray effectively. This is compared to an artisan, an expert carpenter. You give him all the materials which he needs. However, if the tools are faulty he cannot produce that beautiful piece of furniture. Similarly, if the mouth is sullied by improper speech, it becomes a very poor tool for praying to God.

The *Shulchan Aruch*[200] gives us a kind of helpful reminder as to which *krias haTorah* is read before Pesach. In quoting from the *Tur,* the *Shulchan Aruch* writes that this is dependent on the year. If it is a regular non-leap year, the sign is "*pakdu u'pischu.*" *Pakdu*, explains the *Mishnah Berurah*, means *tzav* (command), meaning that in this case we read *Parshas Tzav* before Pesach. During a leap year, the sign is "*sigru u'pischu.*" *Sigru* comes from the *metzora*, who is the *musgar*, known as such because he is closed off from society. Speaking badly caused him to be shut off from all human contact, and he needs to learn his lesson. *Sigru u'pischu* is thereby the prerequisite for your *yetzias Mitzrayim*, leaving Egypt. It is for this reason that we read *Parshas Metzora* before Pesach on a leap year.

What is the source for this?

At the beginning of *Sefer Shemos*, when Moshe Rabbeinu goes out on the second day he finds two Jews fighting. He steps in between them saying, "*Rasha* (wicked one), *lamah sakeh rei'echa* (why are you hitting your brother)?"[201] Instead of their saying Thank you for breaking up the fight, the two men respond to Moshe, "*Ha-le-hargeini atah omer* (who made you the officer around here? Are you

---

200   *Orach Chaim* 428:4.
201   *Shemos* 2:13.

going to kill me)? *Ka'asher haragta es ha-mitzri* (as you have killed the Egyptian)?" Moshe was subsequently afraid and he said, "*Achein noda ha'davar* (now the matter is known)."[202]

The literal meaning of the phrase, "*Achein noda ha'davar*," is, "The matter is known that I killed the Egyptian. Pharoah is going to chase after me. I have to run for my life." However, Rashi brings a *midrash* which explains this phrase in a most powerful way. Moshe Rabbeinu exclaims, "*Oy*! I was wondering all this time, *meh chatu Yisrael*? What did the Jewish people sin more than any of the other seventy nations of the world that they should be subjected to literally such crushing labor? Now, I see that they have among them informers, people who speak badly. I see now that they are indeed deserving of such punishment. *Achein noda ha'***davar*** — literally, the word is known."

We see that everything started with bad speech.

How then did we succeed in getting out of Mitzrayim?

There is a beautiful song, written by Yossi Green, and sung by Yaakov Shwekey, which is taken from the words of the *midrash Yalkut Shimoni* on *Yeshaya*.[203] Says the *Yalkut*,[204] the Rabbis taught that at the time when the *Mashiach* is going to come, he will stand on the roof of the Beis Hamikdash and will call out to the Jewish people, "*Anavim*, you humble ones, you who are filled with humility, the time of your redemption has arrived."

Our *parsha* is read in the Pesach season. There is so much about *Pesach*, such as the matzah, which is low. Our Rabbis tell us the purpose of the search for *chametz* is not merely to search for any *chametz* which might be around. In addition, we are to search for and find the imperfections within each and every one of us. If we are to feel as if we left Egypt we have to create within ourselves the feeling that we are truly *anavim*, truly humble, worthy of redemption. The *gemara* in *Arachin* tells us that among the seven causes of leprosy is *gasus ha'ruach*, haughtiness. It is only a sense of haughtiness which

---

202 Ibid.

203 Ch. 60.

204 499.

can bring a person to speak ill against someone else. Therefore, *Parshas Metzora* teaches us that very powerful lesson of *sigru u'pischu*, be careful how you speak — and then can we truly celebrate the *Yom Tov* of Pesach.

ACHAREI MOS
THE PROPHECY OF ISRAEL

Whenever we read two *parshios* on a Shabbos, the rule is that we always read the *haftorah* designated for the second *parsha*. For example, when the two *parshios* of *Tazria* and *Metzora* are read together, we read the *haftorah* for *Metzora*. The only exception is on the Shabbos when the *parshios* of *Acharei Mos* and *Kedoshim* are read together. The *Rama*[205] in expressing the *Ashkenazi* custom, writes that we read the *haftorah* of *Acharei Mos*. Why is this so?

The *Mishnah Berurah*[206] explains that the *haftorah* of *Parshas Kedoshim* speaks about *to'avas Yerushalayim*, the abomination of Jerusalem and its wrongdoings. There is no consolation. The *haftorah* designated for *Acharei Mos*, on the other hand, is more uplifting. It is a very short excerpt, taken from the prophet *Amos*.[207] The first half of the *haftorah* is fittingly parallel to the end of the *parsha* of *Acharei Mos*, teaching that if we do not live up to our responsibilities

---

205 *Shulchan Aruch O.C.* 428.
206 *Mishnah Berurah* 428:26.
207 Ch. 9.

as Torah-observant Jews we will be exiled from the land. The second half of the *haftorah*, however, is a beautiful turnaround. The *navi* mentions that the possibility exists for all other nations who are exiled from their land to be permanently exiled. As for the Jewish people, however, the *navi* promises, "*Ba'yom ha-hu akim es sukkas David ha-nofeles,*"[208] on that day I [God] will raise up the tabernacle of David which is fallen. There will be a third Beis Hamikdash, says the prophet. And he continues his promise, "*Ve'gadarti es pirtzeihen va'harisosav akim,*" and I [God] will [literally] repair its breaches [I will rebuild the cities], and I will erect its ruins.

Interestingly, the *gemara* in *Sanhedrin*[209] says, "*Ein lecha keitz meguleh mi'zu,*" there is no clearer indication that *Mashiach* is coming than when the Land of Israel will produce its fruit in abundance. The *gemara* then proceeds to quote from the *navi Yechezkel*, "This is for My people, Israel, '*ki keirvu lavo,*'[210] because they are coming."

The *gemara* in *Megillah*,[211] in discussing the particular order of the blessings of the *Shmoneh Esreh*, asks why the ninth *brachah* is *birkas ha-shanim*, the *brachah* of *parnassah* (making a living). Essentially, we ask Hashem for our allowance. The very next *brachah* is where we ask Hashem for *kibbutz galuyos*, the ingathering of the exiles.

Can we not pray for the rest of the Jewish people before we need our own allowance?

The *gemara* responds with a resounding, "No!" When we pray that Eretz Yisrael should be blessed with good produce for the year, it is in order that we will be able to feed *Klal Yisrael* who is coming into the land. Which verse does the *gemara* bring as proof of this statement? It is none other than the same verse brought in the above-mentioned *gemara* in *Sanhedrin*, "*Ve'atem harei yisrael anpechem titeinu u'peryechem tis'u le'ami Yisrael ki keirvu lavo.*"[212] The *navi Yechezkel* makes just this correlation between the blossoming of nature in the

---

208 *Amos* 9:11.
209 98a.
210 *Yechezkel* 36:8.
211 17b.
212 *Yechezkel* 36:8.

Land of Israel and the imminent entrance of the Jewish people into the land. Rashi[213] explains that the fact that the entrance of the Jewish people into the land will occur at the same time as the branches of the trees in Israel bear their fruit indicates that the ingathering of the exiles will occur at the precise time of *birkas ha-shanim*, blessing for abundance in the year.

We can see this in our own day. Open your eyes and see the miracle of what is happening in Israel today. Do not be distracted by important but smaller news items from Israel. Simply look and see the hand of God, which is enabling the land to produce for us. The land did not produce for our enemies for more than 1,800 years.

This is such a powerful concept, which is expressed in quite provocative terms in our *parsha*. It gives all of us not only a special *oneg Shabbos*, but when we listen in *shul* to this very short *haftorah* we should say, "Wow! *Baruch Hashem*, *bli ayin hara*, this is happening right now!" We should use this encouragement and consolation to remain strong in our belief of what is to come, *b'ezras Hashem*, in the near future.

---

213 *Megillah* 17b.

KEDOSHIM
YOU CAN BE HOLY

The verse says, *"Lo sikom ve'lo sitor es bnei amecha,"* you shall not take revenge and you shall not bear a grudge against the members of your people. The verse then continues with *"Ve'ahavta le'rei'acha kamocha,"* you shall love your fellow as yourself, and then concludes, *"Ani Hashem,"*[214] I am God.

Rashi cites the case of revenge by bringing the following example from the *gemara* in *Yoma*[215]. Reuven asks his neighbor Shimon, "Please lend me your sickle," and Shimon says no. The next day, Shimon is in need of something and he says to Reuven, "Please lend me your hatchet." Reuven's response is, "No. You did not lend me your sickle, therefore I am not lending you my hatchet." If this sounds childish, indeed it is. However, oftentimes there is that child in each and every one of us. The Torah is thereby telling us that we cannot be childlike.

"Lo sitor," which is the Torah commandment not to harbor or bear a grudge, is demonstrated by the same case with a slightly dif-

---

214 *Vayikra* 19:18.
215 *Yoma* 23a.

ferent ending. Reuven asks Shimon to please lend him his sickle and Shimon says no. The next day, when Shimon asks for the hatchet, Reuven responds "Sure. I'm not like you. You didn't lend me your sickle, but I will lend you my hatchet." The Torah prohibits both of these cases. Why?

Let us consider three approaches to the prohibitions of not taking revenge and not bearing a grudge.

The most startling is perhaps that of the *Sefer haChinuch*. The *Chinuch*[216] understands the concept of not taking revenge in the following way. The first example was where Reuven says, "I am not lending you the hatchet because you didn't lend me the sickle." In the bigger scheme of things, the fact that Shimon originally said no is because God did not want Reuven to have Shimon's sickle. It is true that Shimon had *bechirah chofshis*, free will. He could have said yes. Maybe he had a bad day. Just Reuven's luck, he happens to ask him on that day. What appears however to be pure happenstance is in reality all *hashgachah pratis*, Divine Providence. Nothing is by chance. God did not want Reuven to have Shimon's sickle. Since God did not want him to have it, Reuven should not be angry at Shimon who was, in a sense, simply doing what was decreed upon Him from on High.

A further illustration of this may be based upon the *Yerushalmi* in *Nedarim*[217] where the *Yerushalmi* compares this scenario to the following situation. An individual is slicing meat, and unfortunately the knife slips and he cuts his hand. Would you think that this person should take revenge by striking the hand which was holding the knife?! Obviously not. So too, explains the *Korban haEida* in his commentary on the *Yerushalmi*, all Jews are connected. We are all limbs of one body. All Israel is to be looked upon as one soul. Even if the right hand hurt the left hand, the left hand is not going to strike the right hand in return.

The Rambam, at the very end[218] of *Hilchos Dayos*, discusses the

---

216   In his 241st and 242nd mitzvah.
217   9:4.
218   Ch. 7, *halachah* 7.

laws of revenge and harboring a grudge. He writes that before one gets upset at someone else one should first put things in the right perspective. People who have their priorities straight understand that such objects as a sickle or a ladder are all *divrei hevel ve'havai*, trivial matters. It is not worth it for a person to bear a grudge regarding them. One's character is much more important. We are commanded to act in a more Godly fashion because we have an obligation of "*ve'halachta bi'drachav*,"[219] literally to walk and to emulate the ways of God. As Hashem does, so should we do. For example, just as He is forgiving, so too is man to be forgiving.

The third approach is that of the Netziv. The Netziv suggests that we look at the verse in its entirety. The verse begins "*Lo sikom ve'lo sitor*," do not take revenge and do not bear a grudge. If you wish to know the reason for this command, simply look to the end of the verse, which reads "*Ve'ahavta le'rei'acha kamocha*," to love your neighbor as yourself. What does this mean? If you need to say no to someone, tell them *why*. You would want to be treated the same way! This is a very refreshing way that we can enhance our interpersonal relationships.

Additionally, the *Da'as Zekeinim*, of the *Ba'alei haTosfos*, notes a very interesting idea which comes from this mitzvah. Let us review the situation again. Reuven says to Shimon, "Lend me your sickle," and Shimon refuses. Sometime later when Shimon asks Reuven to lend him his hatchet, Reuven says, "No. I'm not lending you mine just like you did not lend me yours." According to our Sages, Reuven is guilty of having committed what we know as the prohibition and the transgression of "*lo sikom*," taking revenge. But what about Shimon, the one who in the first place refused to lend the sickle? Why is he not guilty of a sin?

The *Da'as Zekeinim*[220] explains that when Shimon said no initially, he was not being hateful. He was simply being stingy. Perhaps he prized his sickle and he could not bear the risk of any damage

---

to it. There is no transgression in this act. God does not force a person to lend his possessions against his will. Reuven, on the other hand, has no qualms about lending out his hatchet. His refusal to lend it only stemmed from his hostile feelings towards Shimon and the accompanying childlike urge to exact revenge on him. To such a person, Hashem says that the love that you have for Me, as the verse concludes "*Ani Hashem*," should overcome the hatred which you have for your fellow.

These are only some of the many challenging *mitzvos* in *Parshas Kedoshim*. The Torah is telling us that we *can* be big, and, please God, we *will* be big. This is a beautiful application of what it means to be *kadosh*.

EMOR
IT STARTS WITH THE CHILDREN

The Torah says, *"Ve'lo sichalelu es sheim kodshi ve'nikdashti be'soch Bnei Yisrael."*[221] You shall not desecrate My holy name. Rather, God commands that He should be sanctified among the Children of Israel.

Rav Yaakov Kamenetsky *zt"l*, in his *sefer Emes Le'Yaakov*, notes something most interesting about this verse. The Torah does not command in the positive form, *takdishu es shmi*, meaning you are to sanctify My name. Rather, the Torah uses the *nif'al* (passive) form, *ve'nikdashti*, that I may be sanctified. Rav Kamenetsky develops a very interesting thesis as a result of this unusual choice of language.

Rav Yaakov quotes the fifth chapter of the Rambam's *Yesodei haTorah*, where the Rambam begins the chapter as follows:

---

221 *Vayikra* 22:32.

> *Kol beis Yisrael metzuvim al Kiddush haSheim ha-gadol ha-zeh, she'ne'emar "ve'nikdashti be'soch Bnei Yisrael."*[222]
>
> The entire house of Israel is commanded regarding the mitzvah of sanctifying God's great name, as it is said (thus quoting the verse from *Parshas Emor*), and I shall be sanctified amidst the Jewish people.

Rav Yaakov explains that the term *kol beis Yisrael* comes to include even children[223] and concludes that this mitzvah is different from all other *mitzvos* in the Torah. In other *mitzvos*, a child is not commanded from the Torah. Rather, the parent has the responsibility of the mitzvah of *chinuch*, of educating and training the child when they are young to perform the *mitzvos* which they will be doing when they become *bar* and *bas mitzvah* and beyond. Here, however, even children are commanded regarding this mitzvah.

We pray it shall never happen again, yet throughout our history of terrible persecution, adults were prepared and actually gave their lives rather than forsake their religion. It is understandable, says Rav Yaakov, that adults could do this. After all, they are commanded in the mitzvah of *kiddush Hashem*. This means that for three sins (idolatry – which includes betraying one's religion, bloodshed and immorality) one has to be prepared to give one's life. Indeed, we say in the *Shema* twice a day, *"be'chol levavcha u've'chol nafshecha,"*[224] that we are to be prepared to give even our lives for God.

But how do parents have the license to offer their children *al kiddush Hashem*, for the sanctification of God's name?

The answer is that it is based upon this verse here in *Parshas Emor*. If, God forbid, the children would have been handed over to

---

222 *Rambam, Mishneh Torah, Hilchos Yesodei haTorah* 5:1.

223 He brings proof of this from the familiar verse in *Hallel*, where we recite *"Yivareich es beis Yisrael… ha-ketanim im ha-gedolim"* (*Tehillim* 115:12-13) — He shall bless the entire house of Israel, the young together with the elderly.

224 *Devarim* 6:5.

another religion, this would have resulted in a terrible *chilul Hashem*. When it comes to this mitzvah, it is not necessarily the positive act about which we are concerned. It is rather the result. Thus, it affects children as well.

Abaye quoted[225] the familiar verse, *"Ve'ahavta es Hashem Elokecha,"*[226] which means literally you are to love Hashem your God, and explained that it does not only refer to loving God. Rather, the name of Heaven should become beloved through you. Ideally, one should become identified with Torah. In addition, his dealings with people should be in a pleasant fashion. What do people say about such a person? "Fortunate are his parents who taught this child Torah. Fortunate is his teacher, who taught him Torah." When an adult conducts himself in a proper way, he thereby becomes a walking *kiddush Hashem*.

Rav Yaakov is teaching us is that this is true for children as well. Children have the capacity and opportunity to sanctify the name of God. We are speaking about the way our children play. Their language has to be significantly different than the inappropriate language which too often one hears in the streets and in the parks. This is not the way a Jewish boy and girl speak. Others should be able to look at the manner in which they play with one another and say, "Look at how special these children are."

This can happen. Consider a story which happened on the bus on Rechov Sorotzkin in Eretz Yisrael. Many schoolchildren got on the bus and were standing at the front to get their tickets punched. As each child's ticket was punched, he moved to the back of the bus. One child was standing there, and the bus driver said, "Move! Go to the back!" The child said, "No, I can't." The bus driver then said, "Why not?" The child explained, "Because you didn't punch my ticket." The driver said, "Yes, I did." The boy said, "No, you did not." The driver angrily repeated, "Move!" And the boy reluctantly went to the back of the bus. A few moments later, the bus driver looked into the

---

225 *Yoma* 86a.
226 *Devarim* 6:5.

mirror and he saw the young boy crying in the back of the bus. The driver stopped the bus, walked to the back and he asked the child, "What's wrong?" The boy said, "This is forbidden. This is theft. I can't ride the bus. It's stealing." And he held out his card. The bus driver punched the card again and patted the boy on the head. This little seven-year-old, unbeknownst to him, did such a beautiful act of *kiddush Hashem*.

This is what we are to learn. We have to train our children, for example, that when they enter a building they should look and see if there is an adult behind them, and if there is, they should hold the door for them. We have to train our children that they dare not call adults twenty or more years older than they are by the adult's first name. This is the element of respect which we have to ingrain in our children.

We are to understand the tremendous responsibility and the tremendous potential which the Torah puts upon *na'arei Bnei Yisrael*. We do not simply teach children now so that they will have good manners when they grow up. The verse is teaching us that these children have the opportunity to make a *kiddush Hashem* right now while they are still young.

With God's help, we will inspire our children accordingly such that we, men, women, *and* children, can strive to fulfill *ve'nikdashti besoch Bnei Yisrael* in the most complete manner which Hashem commanded.

BEHAR
A LAND WITH A MIND OF ITS OWN

The primary *mitzvos* in our *parsha* are the *mitzvos* of *shmittah* and *yovel*. Succinctly put, the Torah says that the Land of Israel is unique. In other places throughout the world, man is familiar with the concept of crop rotation: man will work the land one year and allow it to lay fallow the next year, in order for the increase of productivity to set in. In the Land of Israel, however, the land has a nature of its own. The farmer is to work the land for six years and the seventh year he is to allow it to remain fallow. He does not plant or sow in the seventh year. Rather, in the seventh year, his field, which has been his personal and private property (and has a sign in front of it saying, "No Trespassing") now becomes public. Anyone can come in and take the produce of the field. *Shmittah* has little to do with crop rotation, as we will see.

There are so many different aspects to this mitzvah. The *Chinuch*[227] identifies three basic tenets of the mitzvah of *shmittah*. First, it serves to reinforce the concept of *chiddush ha'olam*, that God is the

227 *Parshas Mishpatim*, mitzvah 84.

Creator. We are reminded of the fact that what the land is providing for us the first six years comes from Him as well. After all, look what is expected to happen in the sixth year — the Torah tells us that there is going to be a blessing. This blessing will take the form of a three-fold yield of produce. This is something which is nothing less than incredible.

As the verse says, *"ki li ha-aretz,"*[228] the Land belongs to Me. You, the farmer, and you, the Jewish people, are not the masters of your land. Rather, God is the Master of the land.

Second, the mitzvah of *shmittah* is to help man acquire the positive character trait of sharing. This is illustrated practically by assisting him in attaining the ability of opening up his land and sharing it with the rest of society.

Third, the mitzvah of *shmittah* serves to increase within the Jewish nation the concept of *bitachon* (trust) and faith in God that He will provide for them in the *shmittah* year.

Interestingly, the opening verse of *Parshas Behar* tells us that the laws of *shmittah* were given to Moshe at Har Sinai. Rashi asks the obvious question: Why does the Torah particularly connect *shmittah* with Har Sinai? Were not all the *mitzvos* of the Torah given at Sinai? Rashi's answer is troublesome in its own right. Rashi says that just as all the details of *shmittah* were given at Sinai, so too the details of all the other *mitzvos* of the Torah were given at Sinai as well. This once again begs the following question: Why specifically was *shmittah* put together with Har Sinai?

Let us consider a possibility. All of us have hopefully visited or plan to visit the Land of Israel. When we plan our itinerary, there are certain places which are paramount. For example, we are going to go to the Kotel. We are going to go, please God, to Kever Rachel (Tomb of Rachel). We will go to Chevron (Hebron). We go to the places where our history was forged and our people became a nation.

How many of us, however, have ever visited Mount Sinai? True, we do not have, with definitive accuracy, the exact location of Mount

---

228 *Vayikra* 25:23.

Sinai. However, even if we were to locate it, Mount Sinai has no sanctity today. While the greatest event in world history occurred there, today it has absolutely no *kedushah*. Why? Perhaps because the Jewish people were passive at Mount Sinai, while God was the active one. In addition, Mount Sinai was only a means for the Torah to be given. The Torah applies everywhere, while Mount Sinai has no lasting holiness.

The Seforno understands the verse where the Torah promises that you will "*achaltem la'sova*,"[229] that the land will yield its produce and you will eat your fill, to mean that the miracle of the sixth year will ideally be that a person is going to eat less than usual. However, this is not because he or she is specifically saving the food because it has to last for three years. Rather, they are going to *naturally* eat less. This smaller amount of food will not only nourish them and give them the vitamins and nutrients which they need, but will completely satiate them. This is the ideal blessing which the sixth year is going to yield. One will not have to work any harder to harvest any more than he would normally.

The Torah, however, continues in the next verse as follows. "*Ve'chi somru ma nochal ba'shana ha-shviis*," and lest you will ask, what will we eat in the *shmittah* year [because after all we will not be planting]? The Torah immediately responds, "*Ve'tzivisi es birchasi lachem*," God says, "And I will command My blessing to you in the sixth year and it will literally cause the grain to increase three-fold." This is an incredible blessing such that after working the land for so many years one gets three times the amount.

How is it possible for the Torah to tell us that, unfortunately, the Jewish people are not going to keep *shmittah* — especially when they see this miracle in front of their very eyes?

The answer is that the Jewish people are given *bechira chofshis* (free will) at all times. Perhaps man does not want to be told what to do, or perhaps he wants to feel a sense of ownership. No matter the reason, *shmittah* demonstrates to the Jewish people how their

---

229 Ibid., 25:19.

land is tied into Torah. *Shmittah* is the law which shows that special, harmonious relationship between Torah and the Land of Israel.

The Torah calls the *shmittah* year a "*shabbos la'Hashem.*"[230] The Ibn Ezra understands this to mean that just as the seventh day is a *shabbos*, so too is the seventh year. Rav Yaakov Kamenetsky, *zt"l* is therefore moved to ask, what does it mean that the Jewish people did not keep the *shmittah* year? How could they not keep it? The answer is that while they may not have worked the land, they did not make use of the *shmittah* year. As we know, Shabbos is not simply a day to relax. Shabbos is rather a day to catch up on all those opportunities of *ruchnius*, of studying, of *davening*, in such an enjoyable way that a person does not often have a chance to do during the rest of the week. Similarly, the *shmittah* year is an incredible opportunity. In the world of academics the concept of a sabbatical is one which is known for teachers and academicians. Here, there is the idea that the entire nation is upgraded to partake in a sabbatical year, a year of Torah study.

What an incredible *zechus* to be so intimately tied to our Land. The land itself and our Torah have an incredible bond. May we be privileged to be an integral part thereof for many years to come.

---

230 *Vayikra* 25:4.

BECHUKOSAI
DREAM ALONG WITH ME

L ag Ba'omer, the thirty-third day of the *omer*, falls out around the time in the year when we read *Parshas Bechukosai*.

There are several different reasons given for the *simchah* on Lag Ba'omer. Primary among them, as we are taught in the *Shulchan Aruch*, is that on Lag Ba'omer the students of Rebbe Akiva stopped dying.

The Jewish people have been blessed with many role models and heroes. Let us focus on two: a teacher and one of his star pupils, namely Rebbe Akiva and Rabbi Shimon bar Yochai. In *Avos Di'Rabbi Nosson*,[231] we are taught of the incredible beginnings of Rabbi Akiva. Rebbe Akiva, we know from the *gemara* in *Kesubos*, was a shepherd. At the age of forty, he had still not studied Torah. At the age of forty, he decided once and for all, "I want to study Torah." Remember, he didn't know that he would end up living for 120 years. Forty in yesteryear was probably closer to a person of sixty today, as their lifespan was considerably less than it is for the average person today. His decision, therefore, is all the more impressive.

---

231 Ch. 6.

What prompted his decision? He chanced upon a miracle. Not a miracle such as Moshe at the burning bush, but Rabbi Akiva chanced upon a rock. He noticed a hole, which had been borne through the rock. He asked, "Who could make the hole?" As he was looking, he noticed a drop of water fall upon the rock. Again and again, another and another drop would fall. He said, "If this soft drop of water can penetrate this very strong rock, then Torah can indeed penetrate my mind." What does he proceed to do? He literally went with the young children, sat in kindergarten, and worked his way up until he became the greatest rabbi and teacher of his day.

What an incredible lesson Rabi Akiva taught! Indeed, it is a lesson which resonates throughout Jewish history. That lesson is that one should never say, "I cannot change." Rather, just the opposite, as indeed we find in the *Midrash Rabbah*,[232] a foolish individual comes into the study hall and he sees that people are studying and he says, "How do you accomplish this?" They tell him, "We start with Torah, *Neviim, Kesuvim, Mikrah, Mishnah,* Talmud, *halachos, aggados.*" When the foolish individual hears what kind of extensive repertoire there is, he says, "How in the world am I ever going to accomplish all this?" He leaves without ever starting.

The *midrash* then describes how the wise man, on the other hand, starts with *one* law, *one* chapter, *one* page until he is *misayem kol haTorah kula,* until he completes the entire Torah. He does it one drop at a time. The idea behind this is that a person can and must constantly have expectations. One cannot stay the way he or she is. One dare not say, "The way I am, this is me and I cannot change." Rebbe Akiva changed. This indeed is a crucial lesson to learn from him.

The *gemara* in *Yevamos*[233] relates that Rebbe Akiva lost 24,000 students. According to the *Seder haDoros,* Rebbe Akiva was ninety-two years old at the time. This is incredible. Everyone would have said, "It's time to stop and let the next generation take over."

---

232 *Parshas Nitzavim.*
233 62b.

Unfortunately, there was no next generation to take over. Once again, Rebbe Akiva said, "I will do it." This dreamer, who dreamt of becoming a *talmid chacham* and actually accomplished this outstanding feat, said "I dream that there will yet be continuity." What did he do? We are told that he takes five more students, namely Rabbi Meir, Rabbi Yehuda, Rabbi Yosi, Rabbi Shimon, and Rabbi Elazar ben Shamua. Amazingly, we today are the beneficiaries of the Oral Law which has been transmitted by these five great *talmidim* of Rebbe Akiva.

Our Rabbis understand the opening of *Parshas Bechukosai*, "*Im bechukosai teileichu*,"[234] to mean that man has to keep moving. This is implicit from the word *teileichu* in the verse. This is also the very important lesson which Rabbi Akiva taught. One cannot stand still. A person may think that he is remaining stagnant and says, "This is me, this is the way I was last year, this is the way I was five years ago, this is the way I am going to be." No way! Either you go up or you go down. Rabbi Akiva taught us that one has to constantly strive to rise up, up, and beyond.

Unfortunately, as we know, Rabbi Akiva faced a terrible end. He was tortured by the Romans, *yemach shmam*, and died *al kiddush Hashem*. His student, Rabbi Shimon bar Yochai, is the one who, together with his son, had to flee from the Romans. They subsequently spent twelve years in the cave.

Lag Ba'omer is the *yahrzeit* of Rabbi Shimon bar Yochai. Additionally, on this day he revealed the *Zohar*, which he composed while he was in the cave.

The *gemara* in *Shabbos*[235] relates the story of Rabbi Shimon bar Yochai. When he and his son finally came out of the cave after twelve years, they saw people engaged in ordinary activities such as plowing, sowing and harvesting the fields. Wherever he and his son cast their gaze, the object of their vision would immediately be incinerated. They were so infused with spirituality to the extent that they could not tolerate man being involved in base worldliness.

---

234 *Vayikra* 26:3.
235 33b.

Meanwhile, a *bas kol*, a heavenly voice, rang out and said to them, "Have you emerged from your cave to destroy My world? Return to the cave." So, they spent another twelve months — a total of thirteen years — in the cave.

When Rabbi Shimon and his son emerged a second time after the twelve months, they saw an old man on Friday clearly running home. In his hand, he had two bundles of myrtles. They stopped him and asked him, "What is this for?" He said, "It's *le'kavod Shabbos*, in honor of Shabbos, one for *zachor* and one for *shamor*." Rabbi Shimon bar Yochai said, "Take a look and see how precious the Jewish people are and how precious the *mitzvos* are to them!" He changed! Rabbi Shimon bar Yochai teaches us as well that he was able to change. He now understood that man can infuse spirituality into his everyday life.

The idea behind Lag Ba'omer is very important. That is, each and every one of us can dream like Rabbi Akiva and focus on making our own world a better one.

How should we start? What can we do?

Those who have not yet started to go through the weekly *parsha* with *Chumash* and Rashi, available today in English, should start now. If he reaches the third or fourth *aliyah*, then he should make a note in his *Chumash* that he got that far. Please God, he should live and be well, he will resume from there next year. This is something which each and every person has the ability to do.

In addition, even if you have never studied *daf yomi* before, start and see the excitement it is going to add to your life. Do not be afraid to take on something new. The Talmud tells us that Rabbi Akiva's students died during this the of the *omer* because "*lo nahagu kavod zeh la'zeh*,"[236] they did not show proper respect one for the other. It does not mean that they did not hold the door for each other. Neither does it mean that they did not say Good Morning to each other. The *Sifsei Chaim* explains that the language which the Talmud uses of there being 12,000 *pairs* of students of Rebbe Akiva, implies that

---

236 *Yevamos* 62b.

we are talking about 12,000 *chavrusas*. When one *chavrusa* gives an answer better than the next one, when one asks a question, when one has an insight, the idea is that the other one should be happy for his partner's growth. Here, in the case of Rabbi Akiva's students, unfortunately, rather than being happy, they were jealous, they resented one another for their insights. This is not a way for people to interact. This is what we have to learn. It is this which we have to take with us from Lag Ba'omer.

Did you ever dream? Did you ever have aspirations? In doing this, we are keeping the great Rebbe and the great *talmid* alive, Rebbe Akiva and Rebbe Shimon bar Yochai. From them, may we all draw the great strength of *chazak chazak ve'nischazek*.

BAMIDBAR
LOVING REBUKE

In the beginning of the third chapter of *Sefer Bamidbar*, the Torah tells us *"Ve'eileh toldos Aharon u'Moshe,"*[237] these are the offspring of Aharon and Moshe. The Torah proceeds to say in the very next verse, *"Ve'eileh Shemos bnei Aharon,"* these are the children of Aharon.

Rashi comments on the spot that the Torah does not mention the children of Moshe, even though the introductory verse cited above did so. Rashi learns from this apparent discrepancy that because Moshe taught his nephews Torah, they are called Moshe's children. This thereby comes to teach us that whoever is privileged to teach his friend's children Torah, the Torah looks upon this act as if he himself had fathered these children.

Consider a delicious story which occurred approximately 100 years ago. Though our lives have changed much since then, the message of the story is still very relevant.

The story[238] begins with a *chosson* (bridegroom), who gets up to

---

237 *Bamidbar* 3:1.
238 See Rabbi Yitzchak Zilberstein's *sefer Ve'ha'arev Na*.

speak on the occasion of his *le'chaim*, whereby people come to meet the *chosson* and the *kallah* and express their well wishes. He gets up and he thanks, first and foremost, God for bringing him to this day and for giving him such a special *kallah*. He then thanks his parents and the parents of the *kallah* for the very special devotion which they have afforded and provided their children, and for bringing them to this moment. He thanks his teachers for educating him and supporting him. Finally, he says, "I want to thank my second-grade teacher." This caught everyone a bit by surprise, as most people do not recall nor do they give special recognition to their second-grade teacher.

"Allow me to explain," said the *chosson*. "Most of the children in my second-grade class came from poor families. That was the demographics of the school which I attended. There was, however, one boy in the class, who came from an exceedingly wealthy family. Imagine, at a time when a second-grader is seven years old and most of us did not have any kind of watch, this young boy received a gold watch for his birthday. He wore it and brought it to school. And, as fitting a seven-year-old, he would take it off and leave it on his desk. One day, he went to the washroom, and when he came back, lo and behold, the watch was not on his desk. 'Rebbe,' he called out, 'my watch is missing!' At that point, the Rebbe had no choice. He asked all twenty-five boys in the class to stand up and put their hands by their sides. He went from boy to boy and put his hand in their pockets.

"When the Rebbe was approaching me," said the *chosson*, "my heart was racing because I knew he would find the watch. The Rebbe found the watch in my pocket. He took it out, and almost like a magician, he literally moved it up his sleeve in such a way that none of the other boys noticed and he immediately went on to the other boys in the class. When he finished going through all twenty-five, he said, 'Fellas, sit down.' He continued, 'I want you to know I have the watch. But I'm going to tell you that no one in this class stole it. What happened was, the *yetzer hara* came and one of the very best boys in the class was not strong enough to overpower it this time. So just this time, he gave in to the *yetzer hara*. But I'm convinced that next time, he and all of the other boys in the class will be able to overcome the *yetzer hara*.'"

Said the *chosson*, "Could you imagine what would have happened to me had the Rebbe identified me as the *ganav* (thief)? Who knows what kind of a negative effect this would have had upon me, not just because of the momentary humiliation for me and my family but for years to come believing that I was a bad boy? The Rebbe did just the opposite. He built me up, and for this I am forever grateful." And so he gave special recognition to the Rebbe at this time, on the occasion of his *le'chaim*.

What an important message and lesson this is for all of us, who serve as teachers or parents. What a difference we can make in the lives of the children! Notice the difference between a good teacher and an outstanding teacher. The idea is that the purpose of all kinds of *tochachah* (rebuke, punishment) is only to bring out the best within the child. The Torah, in *Parshas Kedoshim*, commands "*Hochei'ach tochiach es amisecha*,"[239] literally, you are to rebuke. This is immediately followed by the way you are to rebuke — "*Ve'lo sisa alav cheit*," make sure that you do not commit a sin in your "piety" by embarrassing him in the process. You must ensure as well that verse 17, which commands the mitzvah of *tochachah*, of rebuke, leads up to verse 18, where the Torah says, "*Ve'ahavta le'rei'acha kamocha*," to love your neighbor as yourself. The goal of rebuke is to lift the person up, not crush them down.

In the ninth chapter of *Mishlei* (Proverbs), the wise King Solomon says, "*Al tochach letz pen yisna'eka hochayach le'chacham ve'yehaveka*."[240] Translated literally, this verse means, do not rebuke a scoffer lest he hate you, rebuke a wise man and he will love you. The Rabbis, however, point out a different *p'shat* in this verse, as indeed is found in the *sefer Menachem Tzion* by the late Rav Menachem

239 *Vayikra* 19:17.
240 *Mishlei* 9:8.

Benzion Zaks, *zt"l*. Do not rebuke someone by calling him or her a *letz*. Do not rebuke them by putting them down. If you do so, *pen yisna'eka*, they will come to hate you (and they will hate the system as well). Rather, *hochach le'chacham*, rebuke and point out how special they are, how good they are, and how unbefitting their character this is. As a result, hopefully, *ve'yehaveka*, they will come to love you.

What a very important and powerful life lesson this is. This is true in terms of the personal interaction which we have with individuals.

Let us conclude with a *mishnah* in *Pirkei Avos*[241] which relates to one's outlook on life. The *mishnah* lists the ten miracles which took place in the Beis Hamikdash and, by extension, in Yerushalayim. We'll focus on the last one.

Picture the scene, which we will, please God, very speedily in our days, be privileged to see again. Hundreds of thousands, if not more, individuals came to Yerushalayim on Pesach, Shavuos and Sukkos. We would imagine that people would complain how crowded it was. Therefore, the *mishnah* teaches us: "*Ve'lo amar adam la'chaveiro tzar li ha-makom she'alin be'Yerushalayim,*"[242] no one said to his neighbor the space is too tight for me to stay overnight in Yerushalayim.

The Chasam Sofer, *zt"l*, explains that of course there was very little room. However, *ve'lo amar adam* comes to teach that they did not focus on the negative. They were able to see in Yerushalayim only the positive.

May we be privileged to see the positive in each and every individual and, please God, in *Yerushalayim bimheira be'yameinu*, speedily in our days. *Amen.*

---

241 Ch. 5.
242 *Pirkei Avos* 5:7.

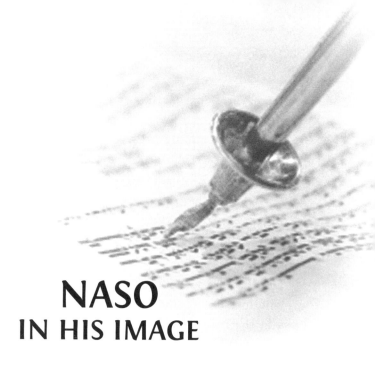

NASO
IN HIS IMAGE

W e all know that there is not one extra word or even one extra letter in the Torah. Yet, the Torah devotes no less than seventy-seven verses to the offering brought by the *nesiim* (princes) at the *chanukas ha-mizbei'ach* (dedication of the altar). The Torah describes the same exact *korban* brought by each of the twelve *nesiim* in the same exact words as well as with the same exact melody no less than twelve times in succession. The Torah could have written the specific *korban* of Nachson ben Aminadav, the prince of the tribe of Judah, and then proceed to tell us that the eleven other princes brought the same exact *korban*. Why the need for such excessive repetition?

The Ramban[243] explains that God did this to extend honor and dignity to His creatures, and especially those who fear him. Had the Torah merely described for us the *korban* of Nachson and subsequently said that the others brought a similar offering, it would have been a slight to their dignity.

---

243 *Ramban Bamidbar* 7:2-5.

Moreover, continues the Ramban, the *nesiim* (princes) extended *kavod* one to another by agreeing to bring an identical *korban* and not to outdo one another.

This whole section of the Torah is proclaiming two words: *Kevod ha'adam*, the dignity of man, the level of reverence at which one is to hold each individual. This teaches us how important it is to extend *kavod* to other people.

Shavuos falls out around the time when we read *Parshas Naso*. A strong theme of the *chag* is *kavod ha'adam*, literally the dignity of man, the same theme we've been discussing in our *parsha*. What does Shavuos have to do with the dignity of man?

First, the *Yalkut Shimoni*[244] says, in the name of Rabbi Levi, that Hashem showed *kavod* to each and every individual at Sinai by communicating with each person on his or her level.

Second, if you look at chapter 23 of *Vayikra*, the *parsha* of the *mo'adim*, you'll note that it is quite a long chapter. Yet, the Torah is consistent and presents in chronological order each holiday and its unique mitzvah. There are no extraneous *mitzvos* mentioned in this chapter.

Except for the last section on Shavuos. The last verse of the Torah's description of the holiday of Shavuos contains the *mitzvos* of *pe'ah*, *leket* and *shichichah*, which means leaving the corner of the field and the gleanings of the harvest for the poor,[245] even though these *mitzvos* were already taught in *Parshas Kedoshim*.[246] Why were they repeated here?

Rav Moshe Feinstein, *zt"l*, in his *Darash Moshe*, explains that this is meant to teach us how we have to give *kavod* to the *ani* (poor person) and the *ger* (proselyte). They are created in the image of God, and deserve respect.

Another *midrash*[247] expounds on the verse, *"Ve'Yosef hurad Mitzraima,"*[248] when Yosef was brought down to Egypt. To what may

244 *Parshas Yisro,* 266.
245 See *Vayikra* 23:22.
246 Ibid., 19:9.
247 *Yalkut, Bereishis* 145.
248 *Bereishis* 39:1.

this be compared, asks the *midrash*? It may be compared to an animal being brought to the market. It does not want to go. To cause it to go, they lead its child before it. The animal then follows its child willfully. Similarly, says the *midrash*, God told Avraham, "*Yado'a teida ki ger yi'hiyeh zaracha be'eretz lo lahem,*"[249] thereby hinting to the enslavement of the Jewish people in Egypt.

God said, "Yaakov has to go down to Egypt. He could and, if necessary, will be brought down in chains in the form of imprisonment because the prophecy must be actualized. But, am I going to bring Yaakov down in a demeaning way? I'm going to cause and orchestrate history in such a way that his son is going to be there in Egypt. And he, in turn, will descend to Egypt in order to see his son."

Incredible! Hashem moved heaven and earth to orchestrate that Yosef be sold. He would become the viceroy in Egypt — in order that Yaakov should go down to Egypt *be'kavod*, in an honorable way.

The late Rabbi Yehuda Zev Segal, *zt"l*, the Manchester Rosh Yeshiva, when he was already an elderly man once visited a certain community. He had visitors all day and well into the night, and by 10 P.M. his host insisted that he call it a night and finally eat something.

As he was being taken home, he noticed a van of yeshiva students pulling out of the driveway. He said to his host, "You sent them away?" His host said, "Yes. I know how hard of a day you had." Said the Rosh Yeshiva to his host, "Tell me, if it was a millionaire coming to give a handsome donation to the yeshiva, would you send him away? Probably not." He continued, "These *bochurim*, these boys, they learn Torah. They are millionaires to *Klal Yisrael*." And he ran after the van, calling, "Millionaires, millionaires! Come back!"

In the end, he met the millionaires, the yeshiva students, for well over an hour. This is *kevod ha'adam*, an old man giving honor to young students. There is no generation gap, when it comes to *kevod ha'adam*. We must teach our children to give *kavod* to their peers and especially to their elders.

---

249 Ibid., 15:13.

All of this comes from the repetition — eleven times — of the *parsha* of the *nesiim* in this week's Torah reading. What a powerful message Hashem is teaching us: Each and every individual deserves his or her due honor, as one of His creations, *kevod ha'adam*.

BEHA'ALOSECHA
BEYOND THE LETTER OF THE LAW

In our *parsha*, right before *"Va'yehi binso'a ha'aron,"*[250] right before the actual carrying of the ark, we are about to go into Eretz Yisrael, and Moshe speaks to his father-in-law. He says, *"Nos'im anachnu"*[251] — we are travelling. One can actually feel the electricity in the air when those words are said! We are going to the place *"asher amar Hashem oso etein lachem,"* we are going to the Promised Land.

Moshe then asks his father-in-law, *"Lecha itanu,"* come with us, *"ve'heitavnu lach,"* and it will be good for you, *"ki Hashem diber tov al Yisrael,"* because God has spoken good concerning Israel. Yisro, however, responds in the negative. *"Lo eileich ki im el artzi ve'el moladeti eileich,"*[252] I am not coming as I am going back to my land and to my family.

Moshe persists, and a second time says to his father-in-law, *"Al*

---

250 *Bamidbar* 10:35.
251 Ibid., 10:29.
252 Ibid., 10:30.

na ta'azov osanu," do not forsake us. Why? Moshe explains, "*Ki al kein yadata chanoseinu bamidbar ve'hayisa lanu le'einayim*,"[253] inasmuch as you know our encampments in the wilderness you shall be to us as eyes.

What a strange verse this is!

Despite the superficial reading, it cannot mean that Moshe is inviting Yisro to be our guide in the desert, because the Torah tells us in incredible detail, "*Al pi Hashem yachanu ve'al pi Hashem yisa'u*,"[254] the Jewish nation camped and they travelled completely and exclusively by the *anan*, the cloud, which was above them. When the cloud moved, so did they. When the cloud remained stationary, so did they. They did not need Yisro to be a scout for them.

What then did Moshe mean?

Rashi explains[255] that when Moshe said, "You shall be for us as eyes," he meant that "you will be as dear to us, literally, as the pupil of our eyes."[256]

If understood correctly, this is an exciting idea. The yearly celebration of *matan Torah*, that incredible moment of revelation at Sinai on Shavuos generally coincides with the reading of *Parshas Beha'alosecha*. The Rabbis tell us in the *gemara*[257] that the Jewish people stood at the foot of the mountain, *tachas ha'har*, literally being underneath the mountain, meaning that God lifted the mountain above them. He then said, "If you accept My Torah, great. If not, this is where you will be killed and buried." On the surface, it appears that the Jewish people at Sinai did not have free will.

The Maharal explains that one does not have to learn the verse literally to mean that God actually lifted up the mountain. Rather, the very experience of God communicating directly with each and every individual in prophetic fashion in and of itself creates the en-

---

253 Ibid., 10:31.

254 Ibid., 9:20.

255 In his third explanation of the verse.

256 The proof text, which Rashi brings for this explanation, is "*Va'ahavtem es ha-ger*" (*Devarim* 10:19), and you shall love the convert.

257 *Shabbos* 88a, based upon the verse, "*Va'yisyatzvu be'sachtis ha-har*" (*Shemos* 19:17).

vironment of *k'fiah*, coercion. They had no choice but to say "Yes, we accept Your Torah." After all, who could possibly refuse the Torah when God was giving it to them directly?

Moshe therefore has a constituency of several million Jews, all of whom were there at Sinai. There was one man, however, who was *not* at Sinai at this time. This was none other than Moshe's father-in-law, Yisro. Yisro was a thinker. Yisro was a person, who *on his own* came to understand and appreciate the God of Israel.

Moshe therefore says to his father-in-law, "Please join us *'ve'hayisa lanu le'einayim.'"* "Do you realize," he says to his father-in-law, "what kind of an example and model you will be to the people?" The people will see that we should serve God out of love, not just ouy of obligation. What a special addition Yisro would have been.

Most of my students are first- and second-year students, between 18 and 20 years old. Every once in a while, a retired gentleman, more than sixty, joins them. It has such a great impact upon the students. They, in a sense, *have* to be there. This gentleman brings a certain sense of seriousness to the classroom. He *wants* to be there.

This is why Moshe was urging his father-in-law, Yisro, to join them. Yisro would bring to the community a very special sense of commitment.

There are three paragraphs of the *Shema*. The first paragraph serves the purpose of *kabbalas ol malchus Shamayim*, accepting upon ourselves the yoke of God's kingship.

The second paragraph, which begins "*Ve'haya im shamoa*,"[258] refers to *kabbalas ol mitzvos*. The Jew thereby accepts upon him and herself the obligation of *mitzvos*.

The third paragraph of the *Shema* is an additional obligation of an acceptance of *mitzvos*, as we say about *tzitzis*, "*U're'isem oso u'zechartem*,"[259] you will see them and you will [thereby] remember all the *mitzvos*.

Rav Soloveitchik, *zt"l* posed the following question: Why do we need two separate, independent acceptances of *mitzvos*?

---

258 *Devarim* 11:13.
259 *Bamidbar* 15:39.

He explained that the second paragraph is our acceptance of *mitzvos* which we *must* perform. The third paragraph represents those *mitzvos* which, although we do not *have* to perform, we *want* to do. Too many of us have heard from teenagers every once in a while, "I don't have to wear *tzitzis* because, after all, I'm not wearing a four-cornered garment. The verse at the end of *Parshas Shelach* states, '*Al kanfei vigdeihem*,'[260] on the corners of their garments, and my shirts don't have four corners."

From the letter of the law, he might even be right. However, true acceptance of *mitzvos* means that we know this is what pleases Hashem. We do not only accept upon ourselves that which we have to do, but we accept upon ourselves that which we want to do as well.

In a sense, this is the theme of *Parshas Beha'alosecha*. Four of the five *mitzvos* in the *parsha* relate to *Pesach Sheini*. There were Jews who were "*temay'im le'nefesh*,"[261] ritually impure, when the time came to observe Pesach. They came to Moshe and said, "We cannot participate in the *korban Pesach* because we are *tamei*."

One would have imagined that deep down they breathed a sigh of relief because, after all, it is technical and difficult to bring the *korban*. But no! They said, "*Lamah nigara*,"[262] we do not want to be deprived. Amazing! They had an excused absence. Yet, they did not want the easy way out. They wanted to get closer because "we *want* to do it not because we *have* to do it."

We must remember Moshe's invitation to Yisro to be a role model for the Jewish people. The *gemara*[263] says that there are times when converts are difficult for the Jewish people. *Tosfos Yeshanim* explains the reason for this statement is that converts oftentimes do things better than the rest of us. They show us up!

This is the lesson which we must learn. We should not become so habituated to our lifestyle that we do things because we have to, or because we've always done so. We should *want* to keep the Torah and get close to Hashem. We should *want* to be good Jews!

---

260 Ibid., 15:38.
261 Ibid., 9:6.
262 Ibid., 9:7
263 *Yevamos* 47b.

SHELACH
DON'T BE SO SMART

The first half of *Parshas Shelach* discusses the sad, tragic episode of the *meraglim*. The people believe the ten spies, as opposed to Calev and Yehoshua. The Torah relates that the people cried that night. As a result, God established that night as a night of crying — Tisha B'Av.

They were about to enter the Promised Land, but unfortunately had their expectations completely dashed. "*Yom la'shanah yom la'shanah*,"[264] the decree against them is to wait for forty years, corresponding to the forty days of spying the land. All males from the age of twenty to sixty would die in the desert.

There are many explanations as to how a people who heard God speak could fall so low, so fast.

Let's focus on the approach of Rabbi Yehuda Leib haKohen Kagan, *zt"l*,[265] who was the *menahel* when I studied at Yeshiva Yaakov Yosef (RJJ) and from whom I was privileged to learn.

At the beginning of *Sefer Devarim*, the episode of the spies is

---

264 *Bamidbar* 14:34.

265 In his *sefer Halichos Yehuda*.

recounted by Moshe, this time with additional details which add to our understanding of what exactly happened. *"Va'tikrivun e'lai kulchem."*[266] Moshe tells the people, "All of you came to me." At this point, Moshe asked God, "Should I or should I not send men to spy out the land?"

Hashem responded, "I told the people that it is a good land."

Indeed, as mentioned earlier in *Sefer Shemos*, God said to Moshe, *"A'aleh eschem mei'ani Mitzrayim,"* I am going to take you out and I am going to bring you to the land which is *"zavas chalav u'dvash,"*[267] flowing with milk and honey.

Therefore, when the people approach Moshe and ask, "Should we go?" Moshe responds, "Hashem already said it is a good land. Hashem is not telling us to go." Since Hashem had already made Himself clear, he stayed out of the issue and gave them free choice to trust Him or follow the spies. Notice that God did not command them to send spies. They wanted to do so: "We'll do it ourselves. We'll go on our own."

The Torah is teaching us such an important and powerful lesson. There is no such thing as doing it on your own. Without *siyata diShmaya* (Divine assistance), man does not accomplish. This is what they learned, and this is what we learned.

There are three areas in which Moshe Rabbeinu acted on his own and God gave him a *yasher koach* for his initiative. First, Moshe breaks the *luchos*, and Hashem says to Moshe, *"Yasher koach she'shibarta."* Second, Moshe separates from his wife, Tzipora, and Hashem approves. Third, Moshe adds another day to the preparation of *kabbalas haTorah*, and Hashem approves.

Meanwhile, when the Jewish people commit the sin of the Golden Calf, Hashem says to Moshe, *"Lech reid ki shicheis amcha,"*[268] Moshe, go down [from the mountain] because your nation has sinned and has become corrupt. Hashem does not say *"the* nation has degenerated." Rather, Hashem says *"amcha,"* your nation. Why? Rashi ex-

266 *Devarim* 1:22.
267 *Shemos* 3:17.
268 *Shemos* 32:7.

plains that Hashem, in essence, is saying to Moshe, "The *eirev rav*, the great mixture of all different peoples, whom you, Moshe, accepted on your own to convert[269] and you did not consult with Me — it is they who became degenerate and they who caused the degeneracy in the others."

This serves as proof that even someone as great as Moshe Rabbeinu, who sometimes acted on his own without consulting God, made a mistake.

Moshe had good intentions. He wanted to do *kiruv*. However, you need *siyata diShmaya*. You cannot do it on your own.

When it comes to business, we need *siyata diShmaya*. We need God's help. Moreover, on the verse, "*Ve'zacharta es Hashem Elokecha ki hu ha-nosein lecha koach la'asos chayil*,"[270] you shall remember God, He is the one who gives you the ability to succeed, the Targum explains that He is the one Who gives you the advice and puts the idea in your mind in the first place. You are not so smart. Hashem has placed this within you. Whatever we do requires *siyata diShmaya*.

This idea is mentioned in great detail in the *gemara* in *Brachos*.[271] When it was time to go to war, the people consulted with Achitofel who would tell them specifically how they were to attack and from which angle they were to attack. He gave them advice concerning the battle strategy. Afterwards, they consulted the Sanhedrin. Rashi explains that they requested permission from the Sanhedrin to wage war in order that the Sanhedrin would pray for them.

Once again, it is *siyata diShmaya*. When the Jews are successful on the battlefield, it is not because we have a better army. It is because we have a better connection Upstairs.

There is one more area in which we need *siyata diShmaya*. That is in the *chinuch* (education) of our children. Of course, we have to send our children to yeshiva. But do not think that the yeshiva can do it alone. There are great challenges that exist in the world at large, and we must try to assist our children face those challenges. Still, don't

269 Reasoning, "Isn't it good that converts should cling to the *Shechinah*?"
270 *Devarim* 8:18.
271 3b.

think that your assistance is what is going to complete the job. The Chazon Ish says that the *yiras Shamayim* of our children, the spiritual development of our children, is dependent on the tears of the Jewish mother when she lights Shabbos candles.

This is *Parshas Shelach*.

It all boils down to *siyata diShmaya*. The *meraglim* thought they could do it on their own. *Parshas Shelach* teaches us that we need *siyata diShmaya* in all that we do. What a powerful lesson to take away from this sad story.

KORACH
BE YOURSELF

After the disaster of the last *parsha*, when it was Divinely decreed that the Jewish people would have to spend an additional forty years in the desert, Moshe's popularity understandably waned. Korach therefore seized the moment to challenge the leadership of his cousin, Moshe. In the process of doing so, 250 great men joined Korach because they wanted more for themselves. They lost their lives. In addition, Korach, Dasan, Aviram and their respective families, lost their lives as well. A plague consumed 14,000 people in *Parshas Korach*. It is not a happy story at all.

By relating the account of Korach, the Torah is not only relating a story of the historical past. The Torah is telling each and every person to look deeply and carefully into themselves and to see how the story of Korach is really the story of (almost) each and every one of us. One has to learn from the mistakes of Korach, and, please God, rise above that which became his unfortunate downfall.

Let us try to focus on one aspect of Korach's character. Hopefully, it will move us to take a quick peek at ourselves. Perhaps we too have just a little bit of what Korach suffered from.

Korach's primary mistake is that he did not realize what he had. He did not appreciate the gift which God gave him. Korach was a *chacham (wise man).* He had prophecy, and saw in *ruach ha-kodesh* (Divine inspiration) that from his progeny would emerge the *navi* Shmuel.

And there was more. Within the family of *Leviim* (Korach was a *Levi*), there were three families: Gershon, Kehas and Merari. Regarding the activities of Gershon and Merari, the Torah uses the term *avodah* to describe their service in the *Mikdash.* The *Ohr Hachaim Hakadosh* and the Chasam Sofer, *zt"l,* note that regarding the service of Kehas, the Torah does not use the term *avodah.* Rather, the term *melachah* is used. The "service" or labor was of a different nature. The nature of what Kehas did was that they were *nosei ha'aron.* They had the incredible privilege of carrying the Ark. The *gemara* in *Sotah*[272] teaches that among the many miracles which occurred during this period of time in Jewish history, was that the *aron* was *"nosei es nosav."* This means that when men were carrying the Ark, it only gave the impression that they were carrying it. In reality, though, the Ark was carrying them. Korach was *mi'nosei ha'aron,* one of the bearers of the Ark.

In other words, he had unbelievable accomplishment and stature! If only he would have realized what he had, Korach could have been truly great. In addition, the *Imrei Emes* brings, in the name of the *Zohar,* that just as we are all familiar with the position of *Kohein Gadol,* which exists in *Am Yisrael,* there was to have been a position of *Levi Gadol* as well. The first to have been able to hold this position would have been none other than... Korach! If only he could have appreciated what he had. Unfortunately, he did not. Because he was always looking over his shoulder to see what Moshe had, Korach could not develop his own potential.

This is the first thing which each of us has to learn. God gave each person his and her unique talent, their own gift. You cannot develop what the next person has and the next person cannot develop what you have. You have to be who you are.

---

272 35b.

The second thing Korach did not learn was that he did not realize who he was not. He did not realize that he was not Moshe. He did not have the capabilities of Moshe. Also, we have to understand that the last of the Ten Commandments, *"Lo sachmod,"*[273] which means literally you are not to covet or be jealous, is not simply a *middah megunah*, a negative character trait. It goes much deeper. If one covets what the next one has, one is actually being *bogeid*, he is actually transgressing and violating the *first* of the Ten Commandments. It is as if he is saying to God, "You, Who controls the world, got it wrong. What You gave the next person, You really should not have given them. You should have given it to me. It is as if You put the money in the wrong account. How could You do this?!"

Let us consider another historical example of this idea. There was an incredibly great man[274] Yeravam ben Nevat, who was chosen by God Himself to be the successor of Shlomo HaMelech over ten of the tribes of Israel. After Shlomo's passing, God wanted Shlomo's son, Rechavam, to reign over two tribes and Yeravam to be king over ten. God would not have chosen him to be king if he hadn't been worthy of the position.

Achiah haShiloni, the *navi*, gives him the honor and presents him with the kingship. Unfortunately, Yeravam ben Nevat is concerned because *aliyah le'regel*, going to the Beis Hamikdash on Pesach, Shavuos and Sukkos, would bring the people to Yerushalayim. As a result, they would see Rechavam, the king of the other two tribes, sitting in the Beis Hamikdash. After all, only a king from *malchus beis David* (David's dynasty) can sit in the Beis Hamikdash. Unfortunately, Yeravam could not live with this jealousy. It possessed him to the extent that we are taught in the Book of Kings[275] that he put a golden calf in Beit El and in Dan, the north and the south of the Land of Israel.

God Himself even invites Yeravam to do *teshuvah*. He says to Yeravam, "I hereby give you and I the opportunity of doing *teshuvah*. And when you do, you and ben Yishai will walk in Gan Eden." Can

273 *Shemos* 20:14.
274 As the *gemara* in *Sanhedrin* 102b points out.
275 *Melachim I*, Ch. 12.

172

you imagine being invited to take a stroll with God Himself together with King David (the son of Yishai)?

Shockingly, Yeravam asks God, "Who is going to lead this procession?" The answer is clearly that God will lead. Yeravam really wanted to know who would be next. When God says to him, "Ben Yishai, David, is going to be second and you, Yeravam, are going to follow David," Yeravam immediately responds that he is not interested. "Thanks, but no thanks, it is not for me," says Yeravam.

This is what we are taught in *Pirkei Avos.*[276] Jealousy removes a person from this world. They do not enjoy what they have. They do not enjoy this world, and unfortunately they lose out on the next world too.

This is why the Torah teaches us about Korach. It is not just history. There is something in this story for each and every person to learn from and incorporate into his life.

---

276 4:21.

CHUKAS
SPRINKLING OF FAITH

Parshas Chukas contains three *mitzvos*,[277] all of which re-
volve around the concept of the *parah adumah* (red heifer)
and *tum'as meis* (ritual impurity caused by contact with a
corpse).

The *parah adumah* is the classic example of a *chok*, a law "without
a reason." The Torah teaches that when an individual has either come
in direct contact with a dead body or was under the same roof as a
dead body, he becomes *tamei nefesh* (ritually impure). A person can
go about his normal, everyday activities while he is *tamei*. However,
he may not enter the Beis Hamikdash nor may he partake of *korbanos*
(offerings). In addition, a *kohein* who is *tamei* may not eat *terumah*. An
impure *Yisrael* may not eat food which is of a holy nature.

How does one rid oneself of this *tumah*? There is only one way.
The person who is *tamei* has the ashes of a red heifer, mixed with
special waters, sprinkled upon him on the third and seventh day of
his counting his week of purity. Afterwards, he or she immerses in a
mikveh, and is considered *tahor* (pure).

---

277 According to the *Sefer haChinuch*.

What is very perplexing is that while purifying the *tamei* person, the *kohein* who administered the sprinkling himself becomes *tamei*! This is something about which the wise King Solomon said, "*Amarti echkama*,"[278] I thought that with the Divine gift God gave me I would be able to understand all of Torah including *parah adumah*. However, says Shlomo HaMelech, "*Ve'hi rechoka mimeni*," this is beyond me and beyond my understanding.

What are we to do with the mitzvah of *parah adumah*?

Rav Yosef Salant, in his *sefer Be'er Yosef*, offers an insightful explanation.

When Moshe Rabbeinu said to God in *Parshas Ki Sisa*, "*Hareini na es kevodecha*,"[279] show me Your Glory, he was in essence saying, "I don't understand the concept of *tzaddik ve'ra lo*." There are unfortunately times it appears that righteous people are suffering. We hear as well, *lo aleinu*, of the suffering of younger people, older people, circumstances which seem to us to be nothing less than tragic in nature. How can we go about our daily lives with such pain and seeming injustice?

The answer is found in the *parah adumah*. Just as we cannot understand this mitzvah, so too God is showing us that we cannot understand His ways. The ways of God are completely beyond that of a human being's understanding. The *navi*, in fact, emphasizes this very message. "*Ki lo machshevosai machshevoseichem ve'lo darcheichem derachai*,"[280] My thoughts are not your thoughts, and My ways are not your ways. Just as the distance between heaven and earth is so great, so too is this gap between God's understanding and ours.

When we had a Beis Hamikdash, the *parah adumah* was a household item. People were constantly in need of it, such as when one's neighbor was sitting *shivah*. People who had the experience of a dead body in their home required the ashes of the *parah adumah* to be sprinkled upon many household articles. As a result, the people were constantly in touch with the idea of *parah adumah*, and it had

278   *Koheles* 7:23.
279   *Shemos* 33:18
280   *Yeshaya* 55:8.

a profound impact upon them. They were just as perplexed by the paradox contained within this mitzvah as we are today. We relate to this mitzvah by accepting the greatness of God.

Rav Shimshon Raphael Hirsch asks, why is it that contact with death makes a person *tamei,* ritually impure? He explains that consciously or unconsciously when a person encounters death, he questions the wisdom of God. There is a shaking of our *emunah.* Therefore, we need the *parah adumah* to restore this belief in our very souls.

There are things which are beyond our comprehension. The *parah adumah* therefore serves as a great source of *emunah,* a great source of trust and belief which we must have in God.

Rashi[281] brings, in the name of Rebbe Moshe haDarshan, that the *parah adumah* was to serve as an atonement for the sin of the Golden Calf. The sin of the Golden Calf was a breakdown in the belief of the people. Therefore, explains Rashi, the *parah adumah* comes to bolster our belief.

May we be privileged very soon by our reading and studying about the *parah adumah* to bolster our *emunah* to be able to truly recognize that it is all *ha'tov ve'hameitiv.*

---

281 Rashi *Bamidbar* 19:22.

BALAK
TORAS CHESED

The *mishnah* in *Pirkei Avos* teaches, "Whoever possesses the following three character traits can be counted among the disciples of our father, Abraham. If someone, however, has the three opposite traits, they are to be counted among the disciples of the wicked Bilaam."[282]

What are the three positive character traits of Avraham? Avraham had a good eye. He had a humble spirit. He also had a meek soul, meaning he was not a greedy individual. Bilaam, on the other hand, possessed exactly the opposite of these character traits. Those who have an evil eye, an arrogant spirit, and are greedy, meaning they are never satisfied with what they have, are of the disciples of Bilaam.

Let us focus on the very first trait, which is a good eye, and its opposite, the bad (or evil) eye. Someone who has a good eye is one who is satisfied with what they have and happy for other people to have valuable possessions as well. The antithesis, the one who possesses the bad eye, is one who is never satisfied with what he has and

---

282 5:23.

resents other people for what they have. This is certainly true in the realm of materialism. People who have a bad eye, even though they may have much, aren't happy if others have more.

Interestingly, this applies as well in the realm of the spiritual. There is an interesting *midrash* in the *Yalkut Shimoni* in *Parshas Yisro*[283] which teaches that at the time when God revealed Himself to the Jewish nation at Mount Sinai, the kings and heads of governments literally trembled in their palaces all over the world. They immediately sent emissaries to Bilaam and said to him, "Is God sending another flood to the world?"

In actuality, the Rabbis based this on *Tehillim* 29, the last two verses of which begin with the words, "*Hashem la'mabul yashav.*"[284] The *midrash* understands this phrase not as a statement, but as a rhetorical question. They understood that something major was going on. They therefore asked, "Is God bringing a flood to the world?" Bilaam responded, saying, "No. Fools, God already swore to Noach that He is not going to bring another flood to this world."

They asked him further, "Maybe He is going to bring a holocaust, a fire?" Bilaam responded again, "No. He is not bringing a *mabul* of water nor a *mabul* of fire. Rather, God is giving the Torah to His people." This is supported by the following verse, "*Hashem oz le'amo yiten,*"[285] Hashem gives strength to His people — meaning He is giving them the Torah.

Once they heard this from Bilaam, the *midrash* concludes, they all fled and returned to their homes. Bilaam unfortunately missed out on an incredible opportunity. He had them all in the palm of his hand. He could have shared his knowledge and changed world history. He had the opportunity to say to them, "Look here. God is giving a very special teaching to the world. He's giving this to the Jewish nation. You don't necessarily have to become Jewish. But look how much you can learn from this. Look at how you can improve your life."

Bilaam had the opportunity at this point to teach, to uplift, and

---

283 Par. 268.
284 *Tehillim* 29:10.
285 *Tehillim* 29:11.

to share, but unfortunately, as we saw in the fifth chapter of *Pirkei Avos*, Bilaam had an evil eye. He did not want to share.

Compare this to Avraham Avinu who had a good eye. The Torah tells us regarding Avraham, *"Ha-nefesh asher asu be'Charan,"*[286] the souls which they [Avraham and Sarah] made in Charan. Avraham positively influenced the men and Sarah positively influenced the women.

Similarly, compare Bilaam to Moshe Rabbeinu. The Rabbis tell us, and Rashi quotes this in *Parshas Balak*[287], that there never was and there never will be another prophet as great as Moshe amongst the Jewish people. However, amongst the nations of the world, Bilaam was, in some way, similar — in order that they should not say, "If only we had a prophet." In any event, we see that there is a connection, a comparison, between the two. Bilaam did not share, challenge or uplift. Moshe Rabbeinu, however, did just that. He was our great teacher, from whom we could constantly learn. For example, at the end of *Parshas Beha'alosecha*, Yehoshua comes and informs Moshe that Eldad and Meidad are prophesying alone in the camp, away from the rest of the people. Yehoshua advises Moshe to imprison them, lest they take away from Moshe's honor. Moshe responds so beautifully: *"U'mi yiten kol am Hashem neviim."*[288] *Halevai*, if only it could be that all Israel could be elevated to the status of prophecy.

Moshe wants to share. He is the conduit, the channel through which Torah is brought to the people. God says to Moshe after the sin of the Golden Calf, "Step aside, and I will make a nation out of you." Rather than express his excitement at this personal *brachah*, Moshe tells God, *"Mecheini na mi'sifricha,"*[289] wipe me out of Your Book, but not the Jewish people. Moshe is Moshe Rabbeinu, who never missed an opportunity to teach and share with others.

The very important concept, which emerges from the contrast of

---

286 *Bereishis* 12:5.
287 *Bamidbar* 22:5.
288 *Bamidbar* 11:29.
289 *Shemos* 32:32.

Bilaam and Avraham and Bilaam and Moshe, is this idea of sharing Torah.

Every Friday night we sing *Eishes Chayil,* which includes the verse, *"Ve'soras chesed al leshonah,"*[290] the Torah of *chesed* is on her tongue. The *gemara* in *Sukkah*[291] asks, is there a Torah of *chesed* and a Torah not of *chesed*? The *gemara* proceeds to respond that a Torah which is shared is a Torah of *chesed* and a Torah which is not shared is a Torah which is not of *chesed.*

Let us conclude with a beautiful *machshavah* of the Apter Rav, the Oheiv Yisrael, who said to his *chasidim* that the concept of *ahavas Yisrael,* to love a Jew, is so important that the idea of *"Ve'ahavta le'rei'acha kamocha,"*[292] You shall love your fellow as yourself, is found in every *parsha.* His students asked him, "Rebbe, what about *Parshas Balak*?" The Oheiv Yisrael responded, "You don't have far to go in *Parshas Balak* to find this concept. In the very opening verse of *Parshas Balak,* *"Va'yar Balak,"*[293] the very name of *Balak* stands for *"Ve'ahavta le'rei'acha kamocha."* His students laughed, and they said, "Rebbe, *Balak* is with a *beis* and *ve'ahavta* is with a *vav,* and *kamocha* is with a *chof* and *Balak* is with a *kuf.*" The Rebbe responded, "If you are going to be so exact, you're never going to come to true *ahavas Yisrael,* the true love of one Jew for another."

This is the time when we remember how the Beis Hamikdash was destroyed at the end of a three-week period because of an unfortunate breakdown in *ahavas Yisrael.* Jews should not be too exact or demanding of each other. The way to increase *ahavas Yisrael* is by the opposite of Bilaam's evil eye, of keeping his spirituality to himself. The Torah which we have must be shared with others. As a result, it will not only earn us great reward, but, please God, inspire all of *Klal Yisrael.*

---

290 *Mishlei* 31:26.
291 49b.
292 *Vayikra* 19:18.
293 *Bamidbar* 22:2.

PINCHAS
SWIM AGAINST THE TIDE

O ur *parsha* includes the request of the five daughters of Zelafchad. They come to Moshe and request inheritance in the Land of Israel. Essentially, the question is whether daughters inherit their father when there are no sons. The answer which the Torah gives them is, "Yes, they do."

The *Yalkut Shimoni*[294] explains that, contrary to appearances, their request occurred immediately following the sin of the *meraglim*, when the decree came against the Jewish nation that they would be spending forty years in the desert. Some Jews cried out, "*Nitnah rosh ve'nashuvah Mitzraimah,*"[295] let us go back to Egypt rather than stay in the desert. It was precisely at this point that the daughters of Zelafchad came forth and said, "Give us land in Eretz Yisrael."

The *Yalkut Shimoni* then teaches that when there is a worthy individual who stands up against an evil or erring generation, that worthy individual gets rewarded twice — once for his acts, and again for all those around him who are not doing what they should be doing.

294 *Yalkut Shimoni Bamidbar* 773.

295 *Bamidbar* 14:4.

The *midrash* gives several examples.

Noach rises up at the same time when "*va'timale ha'aretz chamas*,"[296] the earth is filled with corruption, violence and theft. There was a break-down at the time of the flood. Noach remained a righteous man. He did not only receive the good which was coming to him, but he received the reward which God would have given to all the other members of his generation.

Avraham was known as Avraham HaIvri, the one who went against the tide, particularly at the time of *dor haflagah*, the generation of the Tower of Bavel. Avraham too received the reward which would have been given to everyone in that generation.

Even Lot, interestingly, had this capacity. The *midrash* points out that this was in contrast to the inhabitants of Sdom who were "*ra'im ve'chata'im la'Hashem me'od*,"[297] exceedingly evil and sinful to God. They practiced their code of ethics of "No *chesed* allowed in Sdom." Lot challenged the people of Sdom. As a result, he received the reward of them all.

The *midrash* then jumps to the daughters of Zelafchad. These righteous women also received the reward of the entire generation. Why?

The *midrash* relates that when these women approach Moshe he says to them, "The populace, as a whole, is looking to go back to Egypt and you are requesting a portion in the land." The daughters of Zelafchad, in response to Moshe, say, "We know that in the end the Jewish people will have a hold on the land." *Bnos Zelafchad* had faith, they had *emunah* in Hashem, that the Jewish nation would come to the Land of Israel. The generation's attachment to the Land of Israel was weak and they stepped into the breach. Our Rabbis therefore remember the daughters of Zelafchad in a very special way.

The *midrash* is teaching us a very important point. Of course, each mitzvah is important and judged in accordance with how it is fulfilled. In addition, there is the factor as to *when* that mitzvah is

---

296 *Bereishis* 6:11.
297 Ibid., 13:13.

being fulfilled. For example, is the mitzvah being fulfilled at a time when society is supporting it or is it being fulfilled at a time when one has that strength of character to go against the tide?

We live in special times. *Eis la'asos la'Hashem*, each generation has its own *avodah*. Years ago, we know that people had a great challenge in finding jobs which gave them Shabbos off. Other times, *kashrus* was most difficult. Today, most people can have due employment without working on Shabbos or *Yom Tov*. There is also so much available in terms of kosher food in every variety. What is the challenge of our generation? There are many things we need to work on. Shabbos is still one of them.

To those who observe Shabbos, perhaps the question is how they keep and spend their Shabbos. Shabbos is not simply a day on which we are to abstain from *melachah*. Of course, it is a significant part of the day. It helps shape and gives character to the day. Of course, it is most significant for the family unit. Throughout the week, most often we do not have the time to properly interact and eat with one another. This is a very special part of what Shabbos offers. However, there is and must be more to the day of Shabbos.

Shabbos is to be a day of personal growth. During the week, many people do not have that much time for the study of Torah. However, to let a Shabbos pass by without formal study of Torah with a *chavrusa*, going to a *shiur*, challenging oneself and growing, is unthinkable! The Ben Ish Chai teaches us that one hour of Torah study on Shabbos is equivalent to no less than one hundred hours during the week. An individual truly connects with Hashem through the Torah, and this sweet connection occurs on Shabbos so much more than it can during the week. It is utilizing the very essence and purpose of Shabbos.

In Chapter 3 of *Bereishis*, Adam is told, "*Arurah ha'odomah ba'avurecha*,"[298] the ground and the earth have been cursed on your behalf. The Malbim, on this verse, comments that man has to work in order to keep himself out of trouble.

---

298 *Bereishis* 3:17.

All week long, man is busy working. Now that our society, especially in the United States, gives him a Sunday, it is wonderful that Sunday becomes a day for family. Family is extremely important. Once again, however, this is a time when a person should say, "I'm going to put into my schedule one hour in the morning or the evening." If he sticks to this consistently, it is going to change the day. It is going to change his perspective on what the weekend is like.

We are different, and these times have to especially remind us of this difference. It is wonderful to watch a ball game, but that cannot be the focus of the day.

On a personal as well as on a collective note, we have to try to enhance our Shabbos. If we succeed in this, then, please God, it will spill over to Sunday and to the rest of the week as well.

May this important lesson, which the Torah is teaching us with the story of the *bnos Zelafchad*, be implemented by each and every one of us.

MATOS
DON'T PLAY GOD

God says to Moshe, "*Nekom nikmas Bnei Yisrael mei'eis haMidyanim achar tei'aseif el amecha*,"[299] take vengeance for the Children of Israel against the Midianites. Afterwards, Moshe, you shall die. This is an incredible message. God tells Moshe that his death is literally contingent upon his doing a certain act — going to war against Midyan.

Yalkut Shimoni relates that if Moshe had wanted to, he could have delayed his death by twenty or thirty years, simply by avoiding the war with Midyan. Moshe, however, said, "If God instructed me to do something, I do not have the right to delay." The next verse informs us that Moshe immediately gives the order, "*Vayidaber Moshe el ha-am*," Moshe speaks strongly to the people because they want to procrastinate. Rashi, quoting the *Sifri* as well as the *Tanchuma*, comments that even though he heard very clearly that his own death was contingent on this matter, Moshe conducts this last act of his life with joy. He does not delay.

---

299 *Bamidbar* 31:2.

What is rather challenging is the *Midrash Rabbah*[300] on the *parsha* which relates that God said to Yehoshua, "*Ka'asher hayisi im Moshe ehyeh imach*,"[301] as I was with your master, Moshe, I will likewise be with you. However, if God was truly with Yehoshua the same way He was with Moshe, Yehoshua should have lived 120 years just like Moshe his teacher did! Why then does Yehoshua lose ten years of his life?[302]

When Hashem says to Moshe, "Take vengeance against the Midianites and after you will die," Moshe did not delay for a moment, even though doing so would bring his death. In contrast, when Yehoshua came to fight against the thirty-one kingdoms in Canaan, he feared that doing so would cause him to die all the sooner because, after all, "God will treat me as he treated my master."

Therefore, Yehoshua started to procrastinate in the war against all the various kings of Canaan. It is written in *Sefer Yehoshua*, "*Yamim rabim asah Yehoshua es kol ha-melachim ha-eileh milchama*,"[303] over many days, years, did Yehoshua conquer the various kings. God says to Yehoshua, "Because you have acted thusly, I will therefore shorten your life by ten years." This occurrence inspired Shlomo to utter the famous verse, which we recite every day as part of "*Yehi kavod*" in the *Pesukei d'Zimra*, "*Rabos machshavos be'lev ish va'atzas Hashem he sakum*,"[304] many are the thoughts of man, but it is the will of God which prevails.

This *midrash* speaks to each and every one of us. It says in the most straight talk, "Don't be so smart. Don't try to outsmart the system. Follow the system. Listen to what God wants and don't make your personal *calculations*."

There is a famous *gemara* in *Brachos*,[305] which tells us that Hashem sends *Yeshaya haNavi* to King Chizkiyahu, who is very sick.

---

300 Ch. 22, Par. 6.
301 *Yehoshua* 1:5.
302 See *Yehoshua* 24:29.
303 *Yehoshua* 11:18.
304 *Mishlei* 19:21.
305 10a.

Yeshaya says to King Chizkiyahu, "*Ko amar Hashem tzav le'beisecha ki meis atah ve'lo sichyeh.*"[306] "God has sent the following message to you," says Yeshaya. "Prepare your will because you are going to die and you shall not live."

The Talmud immediately asks, if he tells him that he is going to die why does he then have to repeat "and you will not live"?

The *gemara* explains that the king is going to die *b'Olam Hazeh*, in this world, and he is not going to live *b'Olam Haba*, in the next world. Chizkiyahu the king, who is a *tzaddik*, asks the prophet, "My goodness! What's the reason for all of this? Why am I deserving of such a severe penalty?"

The prophet responds to him, "Because you did not engage in procreation. You did not marry. You did not have children." The king says to him, "Do you want to know why? Because I saw with Divine inspiration," said the virtuous king, "that I would have evil children." Indeed, he was right. He saw that Menashe would come from his progeny. Menashe was a king, who was so evil and idolatrous that every time he saw God's name in the *Sefer Torah*, he literally ripped it out and put in the name of idolatry instead. The king therefore reasoned that it is better to refrain from the mitzvah of having children than to beget such offspring.

The prophet responds back to the king, "*Be'hadi kavshei de'Rachmana lamah lach*?" How dare you concern yourself with these hidden matters, which belong in the realm of God? Rather, what you are commanded to do you must do. This means that if your purpose in this world is to have children, then do it. And what is God's will, He will decide.

What a powerful *gemara*. This *gemara* is to teach us a very important lesson. There are those who literally exclaim, "My goodness! The cost of yeshiva tuition today is staggering. For elementary school in many locations we are paying $15-20,000 per child. Then there is high school, and then you can have expenses of college. My goodness! How can we afford to have more children?"

306 *Melachim* I 20:1; *Yeshaya* 38:1.

Parshas Matos comes and addresses itself to this issue. It is exactly what our *midrash* is telling us. Yehoshua meant well when he engaged in the war with the many Canaanite kings for an extended period of time. After all, the commentaries on this *midrash* say that Yehoshua understood that as long as he was alive, the people would follow God. Indeed, after his death was when everything went downhill. Nevertheless, Yehoshua was still criticized because unlike Moshe, he did not follow through as quickly as he should have on God's directive.

There is a very powerful *gemara* in *Niddah*[307] whereby Rav Yitzchak the son of Rav Ami teaches that when a child is born, his loaf of bread is literally created with him. In other words, God is the one who provides the sustenance. *Parnassah* comes from God. If we unfortunately make the kinds of reckonings such as "I cannot have more children because I won't be able to send them to yeshiva", we are, literally, doubting God's ability to provide. God wants us to have children! How we'll afford them is up to God.

Our job is not to make all kinds of complicated calculations. Our job is to continually try to improve ourselves, our learning and our mitzvah observance. Leave the rest to God. He knows what He is doing.

---

307 31b.

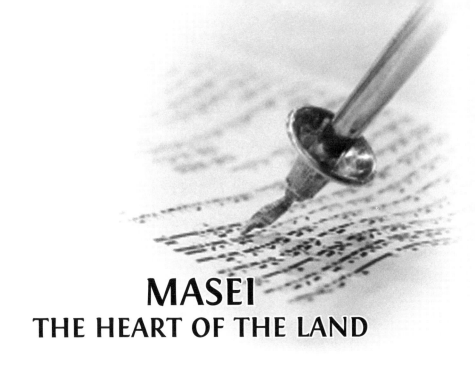

MASEI
THE HEART OF THE LAND

The Ramban sees in *Parshas Masei* the source for what he considers to be the positive mitzvah of living in Eretz Yisrael. The verse in the Torah, on which this is based, is *"Ve'horashtem es ha-aretz ve'yeshavtem ba,"*[308] you shall possess the land and you shall dwell in it.

It is especially important for us to remember this mitzvah at this time of year, as I remember hearing the following idea from one of my *Rebbeim*. In the beginning of the Book of *Eichah*, which we read on Tisha B'Av, it says *"Ve'dimasa al lechyah,"*[309] her tear is on her cheek, in the present tense. The *Nesivos*, in his commentary on the Book of *Eichah*, says that the present tense of this phrase indicates that the sin is still there. The sin of the spies' rejection of Eretz Yisrael is still fresh. We dare not be guilty of this sin in our day. We must recognize and emphasize that Eretz Yisrael is our home. We must also realize that as wonderful as Eretz Yisrael is today, there is something missing. The Land is currently lacking its most important part — the Temple itself.

---

308 *Bamidbar* 33:53.
309 *Eichah* 1:2.

The *gemara*[310] relates that when the second Beis Hamikdash was destroyed there were many Jews who became ascetics. As an expression of mourning for the destruction of the Temple, they resolved not to eat meat or drink wine. They focused on meat and wine in particular because meat and wine were offered on the *mizbei'ach* (altar) as *korbanos*.

Rebbe Yehoshua sought to dissuade them. He therefore asked them, "Why is it that you are not eating meat and not drinking wine?" They responded, "How can we eat meat? It used to be brought on the altar as part of the sacred sacrifices. And now, without a Temple, is it proper that we should enjoy meat while the sacred altar is deprived of it? Certainly not! Furthermore, how can we drink wine when they used to pour wine on the altar and now we don't have an altar?"

Rebbe Yehoshua then responded, "If that's the case, then we shouldn't eat bread because there used to be meal offerings and we don't have them anymore." They replied, "Okay, then we will eat fruit." Rebbe Yehoshua said, "We can't eat fruit either because we don't have *bikurim*, the bringing of the first fruits." So they said, "We will eat other fruits."

"But wait!" he said. "We shouldn't be able to drink water because the special water libation, brought on Sukkos, is no longer relevant."

The Talmud is thus teaching us that while we must mourn for the Beis Hamikdash, to mourn excessively is misguided unless the majority of the people are able to comply with the mourning decrees. Theoretically, we should abstain from meat and wine all year long. However, since the majority of the people cannot do so, the Rabbis said that for this period of the Nine Days from Rosh Chodesh through the morning of the Tenth of Av (excluding Shabbos), it is appropriate that we should do without, in order to remember the destruction.

If we are going to be honest with ourselves, the period of the Nine Days is difficult to relate to because most of us really have a hard time never having seen the Beis Hamikdash.

---

310 *Bava Basra* 60b.

What is it, therefore, for which we are mourning nowadays?

Consider a fascinating *gemara* from *Maseches Megillah.*[311] The Beis Hamikdash was built primarily in the portion of the tribe of Binyamin. Binyamin received this great honor as a reward for the fact that he did not participate in the sale of Yosef. Granted, he was not there at that time. Still, he did not have this stain on his hands. Therefore, he gained the privilege to have the Beis Hamikdash built on his property.

There was, however, a small strip from the portion of the tribe of Yehuda, which was contiguous to that of Binyamin, on which part of the *mizbei'ach* (altar) was built. The Talmud relates that Binyamin, the righteous one, anguished over this each day, hoping to absorb it, wanting to have more sanctity. In other words, Binyamin wanted the *entire* altar to be in the portion of his tribe. The verse in *Parshas Vezos HaBerachah*, "*Chofeif alav kol ha'yom,*"[312] which is part of the *brachah* given to the tribe of Binyamin by Moshe Rabbeinu before he dies, is understood by our Rabbis as indicating that Binyamin agonizes over this constantly.

What is the reward which he subsequently receives?

The Talmud explains that as a consolation for the loss of part of the area of the *mizbei'ach*, Binyamin acquired the privilege to become the host to the *Shechinah*. There are two possibilities as to the meaning of this statement. First, it means that the Holy of Holies was in the portion of Binyamin. Alternatively, it means that wherever the *Shechinah* was, whether in Shilo, Nov and Givon, and finally the Beis Hamikdash, the resting place of the *Shechinah* was in the territory of Binyamin.

We see from this *gemara* that when there is a yearning to have more, this, in turn, enables the person to get more. We should realize that we are lacking without the Beis Hamikdash. We are lacking a certain closeness to God. We are lacking *brachos* which emerge from the Beis Hamikdash. Unfortunately, the Rabbis tell us that so many

---

311 *Megillah* 26a, it also appears in *Yoma* 12a.
312 *Devarim* 33:12.

of the *tzaros* (troubles) which befall us come to us because of the lack of a Beis Hamikdash.

The *halachah* says that the person who experiences a personal loss is not permitted to over-mourn. For example, on the last day of *shivah* the *halachah* dictates that the mourner gets up in the morning because of the concept *miktzas ha'yom ke'kulo*, part of the day is like the whole day. A person may say, "I am self-employed or I am tired and my boss will give me the day off. Let me sit the whole day." Comes the *halachah* and says to the person, "No." A person is not allowed to do more.

Yet, when it comes to crying for the Beis Hamikdash, there is no such thing as over-crying or over-mourning.

What is the difference?

Rav Soloveitchik, *zt"l*, explains[313] that death is part of the natural course of events in this world. It happens to every living being. The destruction of the Beis Hamikdash, in contrast, was an unnatural occurrence. The Beis Hamikdash was much more than a physical edifice. It symbolized the relationship between Hashem and the Jewish people. It was the focal point of spirituality in this world. Its destruction was *not* inevitable.

When we mourn the loss of the Beis Hamikdash, we are not crying simply for the wood and the stones. We mourn the fact that we no longer see Hashem's Presence as clearly as it once was in the world and that our relationship with Him is strained. We long for the day when the Jewish people will reunite with Hashem and feel His closeness once again. In other words, we hope for the day when the world will return to its natural state. It is for this reason that we are obligated to cry on Tisha B'Av.

There is no limit to our crying on Tisha B'Av because the loss of the Beis Hamikdash is a reality with which we can never really come to terms.

---

313 Based on the *Rambam, Mishneh Torah, Hilchos Aveilus* 13:11.

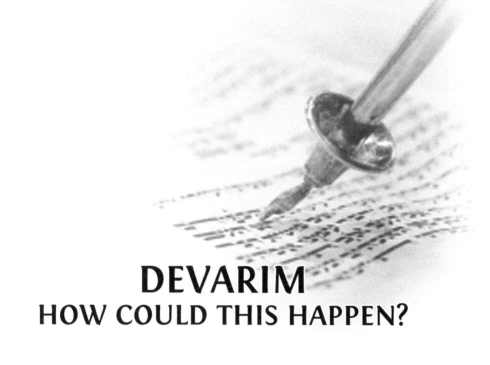

DEVARIM
HOW COULD THIS HAPPEN?

The reading of *Parshas Devarim* every year falls out on the Shabbos immediately prior to Tisha B'Av. This is not by chance. Our Rabbis look at *Parshas Devarim*, its *haftorah*, and the Book of *Eichah* (which we read on Tisha B'Av) and they notice one particular word repeated in all three places. Based on this, the Rabbis deduce that there must be a connection between the events which surround this word in all three contexts. This word is "*eichah*."[314] In simplistic terms, *how* could this happen? More importantly, since it has already occurred, what can we do to correct the situation and restore our days to those of old?[315]

The *gemara* in *Taanis*[316] says, "*Kol ha-misabel al Yerushalayim zocheh ve'ro'eh be'simchasah*," whoever mourns for Jerusalem merits and sees its happiness and joy. We generally translate this statement as something to which we will be privileged in the future.

However, if the intention was to say the person who mourns *will*

314 *Devarim* 1:12; *Yeshaya* 1:21; *Eichah* 1:1.
315 See *Eichah* 5:21.
316 30b.

in the future merit and *will* see the joy and happiness of Jerusalem, then the *gemara* would have used the words *yizkeh ve'yireh*. However, the *gemara* specifically uses the words *zocheh ve'ro'eh*, which are in the present tense. Why is this statement written in the present tense, as if to say that the very act of mourning allows us to see the happiness and joy of Yerushalayim?

We can compare this to something we do on the night of the Pesach Seder. When we begin the section of *magid* and retell the story of the exodus from Egypt, we proceed according to the concept of *maschil b'gnus u'mesayem b'shvach*.[317] We begin with the degradation, "*Avadim hayinu*" and "*Mitchila ovdei avodah zarah hayu avoseinu*." We speak about the negative and only through the negative can we appreciate the positive.

This is what the *gemara* in *Taanis* is telling us our mourning for Yerushalayim should be about. There is a very powerful *midrash*, found in *Bereishis Rabbah*,[318] which demonstrates this idea. First, we need a bit of background information. The *Tanchuma*, both in *Bechukosai* and *Naso*, says that God desired a residence here in this world just as He has a residence upstairs in heaven. The Beis Hamikdash was, in essence, God's residence down here in this world. As long as God's Presence was down here, it was a different world.

The *midrash* in *Bereishis Rabbah* tells us something fascinating. When Adam haRishon sinned, God's Presence left this world and retreated to the first heaven. When Kayin sinned, His Presence went up to the second heaven. When the generation of Enosh sinned, it went up to the third. The *mabul* (flood) brought it to the fourth. The Tower of Bavel brought it to the fifth. Sdom brought it to the sixth. Mitzrayim, in the days of Avraham, brought it to the seventh. The *midrash* then tells us that seven *tzaddikim*, namely Avraham, Yitzchak, Yaakov, Levi, Kehas, Amram and Moshe, brought the *Shechinah* (God's Presence) back down to this world once again.

---

317 See *Pesachim* 116a.
318 19:7.

Our mourning on Tisha B'Av is meant to demonstrate our intense yearning for God's Presence to return to this world.

After the week of *shivah* for Rabbi Elazar Abuchatzeira, *zt"l*, who was tragically stabbed to death, Rav Shteinman, *shlita*, made a very powerful statement. When this *tzarah* befell the Jewish people, it was too painful for words. How could such a *tzarah* have happened? I do not have the answer. No one has the answer.

Rav Shteinman, however, suggested something very strong. He quoted Rabbeinu Yona in the *Sha'arei Teshuvah*, *Sha'ar Shlishi*[319] as follows. One who insults someone else publicly loses his share in the World to Come. Why is it that this person loses his share while a murderer does not lose his share in the World to Come?

The reason for this is because one who embarrasses his friend in public does not recognize the severity of his sin. Therefore, his soul is not so bitter over what he has done. He will thus not feel and relate to his sin as the murderer does. He is literally far from repenting and he does not repent. This is in contrast to the murderer, who knows that he did something wrong and is ready to repent if he so wills.

In the *parsha* in the Torah which discusses the *eglah arufah*,[320] the Ibn Ezra asks: Why does God command that specifically the closest city should perform this ritual? He explains that had the city closest to the corpse not done a major sin, nothing would have happened close to it.

In other words, just as by Chernobyl where, in consequence thereof, there was pollution in the air, we can similarly understand the negativity which is in the environment and the atmosphere. Yerushalayim, at its peak, emits positivity. Right now, because we still have a break-down of relationships man-to-man, there is negativity in the air. This negativity is equivalent to murder. Hence, unfortunately, things which you and I could not have anticipated, we have tragically seen in our day.

---

319 *Siman* 141.
320 *Devarim* 21:1-9.

When we sit down on the ground on the night of Tisha B'Av and remain seated through midday, we have to remind ourselves that, thank God, we have made tremendous strides. There is, however, still a long way to go. It is this train of thought which should accompany us as we enter into another Tisha B'Av and thereby help to make it a truly meaningful fast.

VA'ESCHANAN
DO AS I DO

Parshas Va'eschanan enlightens us with a dozen *mitzvos*. We are met with the *Aseres Hadibros* (Ten Commandments), the mitzvah of *Shema Yisrael*, the *achdus* of Hashem (the oneness of God), the mitzvah of *talmud Torah*, the mitzvah of *tefillin*, the mitzvah of *mezuzah*, the prohibition of intermarriage, etc. What a special *parsha*! The *parsha* itself, I believe, consoles the Jewish people.

Let us consider the first paragraph of the *Shema*.[321] The verse begins, *"Ve'shinantam l'vanecha,"* and you are to teach them to your children. The Talmud teaches that *"vanecha,"* your children, in this verse refers to *"talmidecha,"* your students. The effective teacher is the one who looks at his students as if they are his children. There is an incredible love that a father and mother have for their children. That is the love that a teacher has to have for his students.

The very next verse is, *"U'kshartam l'os al yadecha ve'hayu le'totafos bein einecha,"* and you are to bind them for a sign on your hand and

---

321 *Devarim* 6:4-9.

they are to be a remembrance between your eyes, a reference to *tefillin*. In the first paragraph of the *Shema*, the mitzvah of *talmud Torah* precedes the mitzvah of *tefillin*.

Interestingly, in the second paragraph of the *Shema* these two *mitzvos* appear in the exact opposite order. First the Torah states, "*U'kshartem osam le'os al yedchem*," and you are to bind them for a sign on your hand.[322] In other words, you are to first put on *tefillin*. The very next verse proclaims, "*Ve'leemad'tem osam es bneichem*," and you are to teach them to your children. Note that in this verse, "*bneichem*" refers to one's actual children.

Why is it that in the first paragraph, when discussing the teacher-student relationship, the mitzvah of *talmud Torah* precedes that of *tefillin* whereas in the second paragraph when we are talking about the obligation of a parent to his own children, the order of these two *mitzvos* is reversed?

The teacher has to teach. That is his profession. He prepares lesson plans in advance on a variety of topics, including the mitzvah of *tefillin*. The instruction precedes the actions.

A parent also has to teach. However, a parent teaches, first and foremost, by example. The parent is the role model for his child. Therefore, a parent teaches about *tefillin* by making sure the child sees you, his father, putting on *tefillin*.

There was a certain gentleman who *davened* in the same *beis medrash* as the late Rav Moshe Feinstein, *zt"l*. He would bring his child to the *beis medrash* where he spent a lot of time shushing the child, in order to make sure that he behaved properly. Rav Moshe asked the man, "What are you doing?" The man responded, "I am teaching him how to *daven*." Said Rav Moshe, "Don't shush, just *daven*, and he will learn to *daven* from you."

There is a delicious teaching brought down in *Maseches Kallah*[323] that when Aharon HaKohen died, no less than 80,000 children named Aharon walked after his coffin. The reason behind this inter-

---

322 Ibid., 11:18.
323 3.

esting behavior is that there were many among *Am Yisrael* who wanted to divorce their wives. It was Aharon who caused them to change their minds. Accordingly, there were 80,000 young men named Aharon. Are we meant to imagine that Aharon HaKohen met with each one of their parents? Of course not! Rather, it comes to demonstrate for us that Aharon's very nature influenced people. He was a role model. Everyone should have one, and everyone should be one.

Tu B'Av generally falls during the week following *Parshas Va'eschanan*. The last *mishnah* in *Maseches Taanis* teaches that Yom Kippur and Tu B'Av were among the happiest days in the Jewish year. This is understandably said about Yom Kippur, the day on which we received the second set of *luchos* (tablets), which showed us that Hashem had forgiven us for the sin of the Golden Calf. However, what is it about Tu B'Av which is so special? The *gemara* lists many special things which occurred on Tu B'Av. Let us focus on one such event.

After King David died, King Shlomo (Solomon), as we know, took the reins. When Shlomo died, his son Rechavam assumed the kingship. Shlomo was a most popular king due to his tremendous wisdom and incredible international relations. He taxed the people heavily, yet they accepted it from him. After he died, his son Rechavam had to make a decision. Would he listen to his father's elder advisors and lower the taxes on the people, or would he listen to his younger advisors and tax them more heavily? He made the wrong decision. He listened to his younger advisors, which ultimately resulted in the secession of ten of the tribes as well as the elevation of Yeravam ben Nevat, a righteous individual at the time, to the appointment of king over those tribes.[324]

Meanwhile, Yeravam changed. He thought, "If I am going to allow the Jewish people in my jurisdiction to go up three times a year, Pesach, Shavuos, and Sukkos, to the Beis Hamikdash, they will leave me and go to Rechavam." In order to maximize control over his kingdom, he placed roadblocks and forbade the Jewish people in his con-

---

324 *Melachim I* 12.

stituency from going up to Yerushalayim for the three pilgrimage festivals. Instead, he positioned two golden calves, one in the north in Dan as well as in the south in Beit El, thereby providing his constituents with the opportunity to worship closer to home.

Years later, Hoshea ben Ela, a king of Israel, removed these roadblocks. However, he did not tell peope to go up to Yerushalayim. Rather, he let them choose between it and the idolatry in the north. Therefore, *"Hoshea ben Ela rasha haya,"*[325] he is considered a wicked king. How so? He certainly improved upon the situation left to him! However, that is not what a role model is supposed to do. After all, he was a king of Israel, a position which assumes the responsibility of being a role model. A true role model is supposed to lead the people, show them, teach them and take the initiative. They would have followed him. Hoshea ben Ela failed in this position.

This is an important lesson for all of us. The *gemara* in *Maseches Brachos* summarizes this message as, *"Gadol shimusho yoser mi'limudo."* It is not only significant to study Torah from a teacher, but it is even more significant to spend personal time with your teacher in order to observe how he acts and to learn from his behavior. Please God, his behavior should rub off on you and uplift your way of life as well.

May this *Shabbos Nachamu* be a meaningful one for us all, first and foremost in fulfilling the command of *ve'shinantam l'vanecha* together with *ve'limad'tem osam es bneichem*, being for our children the ideal role models who act in a way which is worthy of duplicating. In addition, even as adults, may our eyes be open, looking always for that person whom we are to follow.

---

325 See Rashi on *Taanis* 31a.

EKEV
EVEN MITZVOS NEED MAZAL

Among the *mitzvos* in our *parsha* is the mitzvah of *Birkas Hamazon*, the mitzvah of reciting Grace after Meals. After one has eaten bread, one is to recite and to fulfill that which is written in the Torah *"Ve'achalta ve'savata u'veirachta es Hashem Elokecha al ha-aretz ha-tova asher nasan lach,"*[326] you are to eat and be satiated, and you are to bless Hashem your God for the good land which He has given to you.

The Chassid Ya'avetz, who was unfortunately expelled from Spain at the time of the Spanish Inquisition, writes[327] that there are certain *mitzvos* which have *mazal*. They are fortunate in that they are fulfilled by our people with joy, enthusiasm and excitement, such as the *mitzvos* of Purim, *bi'ur chametz*, and even *basar ve'chalav* and *kashrus*.

There are other *mitzvos*, however, which are "less fortunate." One such mitzvah is that of *Birkas Hamazon*. Though over five hundred years have passed since the Chassid Ya'avetz wrote this idea, unfortunately, things have not changed.

---

326 *Devarim* 8:10.
327 In his *sefer Chasdei Hashem.*

The Rabbis tell us that there is a mitzvah to eat three meals on Shabbos. This is a rabbinic mitzvah. It is a wonderful mitzvah. It is a mitzvah of *oneg Shabbos*.

A Shabbos meal can oftentimes last as long as two hours. It can be filled with *zemiros*, *divrei Torah*, good food, and certainly one can and one should enjoy the meal. What follows is the *Birkas Hamazon*. The meal took two hours. The question one must ask oneself is: How long does the *Birkas Hamazon* take? We enjoy the meal. Ask yourself though, when is the last time you enjoyed the *Birkas Hamazon*? When is the last time that it was truly a religious and spiritual high?

The Rabbis ask: What vehicle did Avraham Avinu, the very first Jew, use as his instrument of *kiruv*? The verse says, *"Va'yita eishel be'ver sheva,"*[328] Avraham planted an *eishel*. Aside from understanding it to be a specific tree, the Rabbis see the word *eishel* as an acronym for *achilah, shesiyah, linah*. Avraham provided people with food, drink and a place to lodge. Others say that Avraham escorted them. Whichever one's preferred explanation, the bottom line is that after people thanked Avraham for the food, he said, "Wait! Don't thank me, thank Hashem." Avraham Avinu introduced people to God through their thanking Him after they ate. This mitzvah is in our genes, indicating tremendous potential for what the mitzvah of *Birkas Hamazon* is to ideally inspire.

The Talmud in *Brachos*[329] tells us: Rav Nachman teaches that *Birkas Hamazon* is really four blessings, but more precisely it is three plus one. The first three are biblical in nature. Moshe composed the first blessing when the *mohn* descended from the heavens. The words *"Be'chein be'chesed u've'rachamim"* reflect this. Yehoshua established the second blessing of *birkas ha'aretz*. We thank God for the Land of Israel.

The third *brachah* was composed by David and Shlomo. They instituted the *brachah* of *bonei Yerushalayim*. In this *brachah*, we thank Hashem for Yerushalayim, for the kingship of Israel as well as for the Beis Hamikdash.

---

328 *Bereishis* 21:33.
329 48b.

The final *brachah* of *Birkas Hamazon* is rabbinic. We demonstrate the distinction of the *brachos* from the Torah and that from the Rabbis in the *Birkas Hamazon* by saying *amen* after the third *brachah*, "*Bonei be'rachamav Yerushalayim, amen*" before we move on to the *brachah* of "*Hatov ve'hameitiv*," which is rabbinic in nature.

Hatov ve'hameitiv, means that God is good and He extends His goodness. One of the reasons given for the festivities of Tu B'Av[330] is that when Bar Kochba was defeated at Beitar, hundreds of thousands of corpses were laying about. The Romans, *yemach shmam*, did not permit us to bury our dead. For two-and-a-half years, the bodies did not deteriorate or give forth any kind of a foul stench. This was nothing less than a miracle. Two-and-a-half years later, on Tu B'Av, these bodies were given over for burial.

A (somewhat) happy conclusion to a very sad story, but why is this event included in the *Birkas Hamazon*?

The Tzlach asked a different question. He asked: Why do we say a *brachah* for the burial of the victims of Beitar if, after all, the bodies hadn't decomposed? If the bodies were in such good shape, why was burial important? The Tzlach explains that burial is not only for the body of the individual who died, it is also for the *neshamah*, the soul. Therefore, the *brachah* of *hatov ve'hameitiv* is recited to remind us that burial is for the *neshamah* as well.

Similarly, says the *Nefesh Aharon*, people think that eating is for the body. Eating is indeed for the body, but it is also for the *neshamah*. The *Shulchan Aruch*,[331] in discussing the *brachah* of *asher yatzar* which one recites after he or she has gone to the bathroom, quotes the final words of the blessing, "*Rofei chol basar u'mafli la'asos*," God is the One Who maintains our healthy bodies and acts wondrously. He then explains that the wonder is that the body and the soul are together in one unit. God fuses together the body, which is most physical, and the *neshamah*, which is most spiritual.

The *Magen Avraham* comments[332] that the same is true regard-

---

330 *Taanis* 31a.
331 *Orach Chaim, Siman* 6.
332 On the gloss of the *Rama* in this *Siman*.

ing the food which we eat: the *neshamah* benefits from the *ruchnius* (spirituality) which is contained in the food while the body benefits from the actual nutrients, the *gashmius* (physicality) in it.

The *Machatzis Hashekel*[333] cites the verse from our *parsha*, where it is written, "*Ki lo al ha-lechem levado yichyeh ha'adam*,"[334] it is not by bread alone that man lives. "*Ki al kol motza pi Hashem yichyeh ha'adam*," rather, by all which emanates from the mouth of God man lives. The *Ari* understands that "*pi Hashem*" is that which is found in the bread itself. In other words, just as burial is for both the body and the soul, so too our eating is for both the body and the soul. This is yet another reason to take *Birkas Hamazon* all the more seriously.

The *Sefer haChinuch* says that *Birkas Hamazon* is really a *zechus* for *parnassah (sustenance)*. In addition, it is also a kind of *middah ke'negged middah*. The more we realize and appreciate all that God has given us, the more He will, please God, give us in the future.

May the mitzvah of *Birkas Hamazon* receive additional attention to update it into the category of a mitzvah of *mazal*.

---

333 On this *halachah* in the *Shulchan Aruch*.
334 *Devarim* 8:3.

RE'EH
THE REAL RECIPIENT

In our *parsha*, the Torah teaches the mitzvah of *tzedakah*, as it says, "*Ki paso'ach tiftach es yadcha*,"[335] literally, you are to open your hand. Whenever the Torah uses a double language (*paso'ach tiftach* is essentially the same word twice), it is for emphasis — meaning this is *really* important.

Interestingly, the Torah says, "*Ki biglal ha-davar ha-zeh yevare-checha Hashem Elokecha*,"[336] because of this matter, God is going to bless you. The Rabbis, expounding on the word *biglal*, explain that it actually comes from the word *galgal*, meaning a wheel, as in a wheel of fortune. Indeed, if someone has wealth today, he does not know what tomorrow will bring for him or for his progeny. The Torah is therefore saying "*ki biglal ha-davar ha-zeh*," if you give today, it will be beneficial for you or your offspring, should they need it in the future.

Please take note that the Torah says that not only is there a positive mitzvah to give, but there are also two negative *mitzvos* in the

---

335 *Devarim* 15:8.
336 Ibid.

realm of *tzedakah*. These *mitzvos* are as follows. The Torah says, *"Lo se'ameitz es levavcha ve'lo sikpotz es yadcha mei'achicha ha-evyon,"*[337] do not harden your heart and do not clench or close your hand against your destitute brother. What powerful language.

Western society sees charity as voluntary. This is not the Torah view. According to most authorities, Torah law mandates that one give a tenth of one's earnings to charity and, if one is able to, one should go as high as twenty percent. Interestingly, one should not give more than twenty percent, lest he become a burden to the community unless the person is, *baruch Hashem*, endowed with a great deal of wealth.

We have to ask ourselves: What is the purpose and the motivation of the mitzvah of *tzedakah*?

First, it is a fulfillment of *"Ve'ahavta le'rei'acha kamocha,"*[338] where the Torah teaches us that we are to literally feel the pain of the next one. If you were in a difficult situation, you would want to be helped. So help others who find themselves in a similar situation.

In addition, there is a mitzvah found at the end of *Sefer Devarim*, *"Ve'halachta be'drachav,"*[339] that man is literally to walk in the ways of God. Giving *tzedakah* is a form of creating a God-like personality. As the nature of Hashem is to give, man is to train himself to become a giver.

Additionally, there is a very powerful teaching found in the *gemara* in *Bava Basra*.[340] A Roman philosopher, Turnus Rufus, asked Rebbe Akiva, "If God loves the poor, why does He not take care of them Himself?" Rabbi Akiva answered, "The mitzvah of *tzedakah* is to save the wealthy one from literally going to *gehinnom* (hell)." In other words, God could take care of the poor on His own. He does not need us. We need the mitzvah of *tzedakah* for ourselves! Its merit will enable us, please God, to go to the right place after 120 years, as Rebbe Akiva teaches. It may also be, as the Baal Shem Tov says,

337 Ibid., 15:7.
338 *Vayikra* 19:18.
339 *Devarim* 28:9.
340 10a.

that oftentimes God wants to give man blessings in this world right now, but the individual is missing a *zechus* (merit). God therefore sends a poor individual or cause his way. If the individual responds well, he can receive what God wants to bestow upon him.

If we want God to respond to us, to be forgiving to us and to be generous with us, we have to, in kind, act that way towards the poor and needy who come our way. If you see a poor individual coming to your door, do not say to your child, "Tell him I'm not home." Do not close the lights and hide! Giving *tzedakah* helps the giver more than the recipient! If we only realized this, we would look upon the mitzvah of *tzedakah* quite differently.

Interestingly, we find in the *gemara* in *Bava Basra*[341] that Rebbe Eliezer would give a *prutah*, charity, before he prayed. Perhaps he felt that he did not deserve to receive everything he asked for based on his merits alone, and was demonstrating that just as he is giving charity, so too God should reciprocate in kind.

Perhaps there is more to this practice. By giving charity before he prays, the individual is expressing his concern and identifying with the community. Therefore, even if he is not worthy of having God respond to his prayers on his own merit, he now has the merit of the community.

The *gemara* in *Brachos*[342] teaches: Rav Chisda says that before you *daven* you are to walk through (no less than) two doors into the synagogue. Not every synagogue has two doors. Therefore, the Talmud explains this statement to mean the length of two doors. This means that you should not sit beside the entrance, which gives the impression that prayer is a burden and you can't wait to leave. Rather, move into the synagogue.

A *chassidishe* understanding of this *gemara* is that the two doors are found in our *parsha*: "*Paso'ach tiftach.*"[343] Show your generosity of spirit. And when you show your generosity of spirit to others, Hashem, please God, will reciprocate in kind.

341 *Bava Basra* 10a.
342 8a.
343 *Devarim* 15:8.

We are approaching a very special time of the year. Let us learn the very important lesson of *Parshas Re'eh*, of the mitzvah of *tzedakah*, and realize the privilege which we have in giving. When we give, we help others — and ourselves.

SHOFTIM
STRENGTH OF CHARACTER

There is a very interesting mitzvah found at the end of our *parsha* which shows the uniqueness of the Jewish nation. The Torah tells us that there are two types of wars. There is a *milchemes mitzvah*, whereby it is a mitzvah for all to participate in the war, such as, God forbid, if the Jewish nation or the Land of Israel is attacked from an enemy from outside its borders.

There is also a *milchemes reshus*, which means an optional kind of war. This means that if we need to expand the boundaries of the Land of Israel, the Torah tells us that first we are to approach the inhabitants of that land and offer them peace. If they should refuse, the Torah tells us that we are permitted to go to war against them. It is here, that we find that prior to going to war a chaplain stands before the men who are eligible to go to war, and makes the following proclamation.

"*Mi ha-ish asher bana bayis*?"[344] Who has built a new house and has not yet inaugurated it? He is to return to his house, lest he die in battle and another man inaugurate it.

---

344 *Devarim* 20:5.

Second, who is the person "*asher nata kerem*?"[345] Who has planted a vineyard and has not "*chilelo*," has not had the opportunity of tasting of its fruit? He too is to return home lest someone else will enjoy, literally, the fruit of his labor.

Finally, "*U'mi ha-ish asher eiras isha*?"[346] The gentleman who is engaged to be married, but has not yet consummated the marriage, he too is to return home, lest someone else marry his bride.

The *shotrim*, law enforcers of the nation, chime in at this point, thereby adding one more exemption to the list. "*Mi ha-ish ha-yarei*," the man who is fearful and afraid, "*ve'rach ha-leivav*," faint-hearted, "*yeilech ve'yashov le'veiso*," he will return to his house "*ve'lo yimas es levav echav kilvavo*," lest he melt the heart of his brothers like his own heart.[347]

Rebbe Akiva[348] understands the verse to be literal. In other words, to whomever is afraid the Torah says, "Go home and don't demoralize the rest of the army."

However, Rabbi Yosi haGlili[349] explains this statement as referring to one who is afraid of *aveiros she'be'yado*, sins which he has committed. The first three exemptions (the one who has built a house, planted a vineyard or is engaged), are all a cover-up. Really, it is only the one who is fearful of his sins who should turn back. However, rather than embarrass him and proclaim, "All sinners, please return home," the Torah sets up a most dignified arrangement of allowing other exemptions. Therefore, when a soldier goes home, those observing him will say, "He must have either built a house, planted a vineyard or is engaged."

Can you imagine any other army in the world sending away able-bodied men because they are somewhat faulty in character? Since when do sins — even "ritual ones," and according to some, even violations of Rabbinic law — affect a soldier's fighting ability?

---

345 Ibid., 20:6.
346 Ibid., 20:7.
347 Ibid., 20:8.
348 *Sotah* 44a.
349 Ibid.

The Torah teaches us that it is not the strength of the soldiers which will ultimately cause the victory. Rather, the victory comes only from Hashem. Therefore, in order to accomplish this we need to create an environment in which God is welcome and comfortable, namely, in the presence of the righteous. In reality, we do not need anyone to go to war. God can do it for us. However, He tries to minimize the outward appearance of His miracles, and we therefore send soldiers with weapons to fight. In truth, however, it is our strength of character that brings God's blessing of victory — not the strength of our muscles.

Our soldiers are our most pious individuals! What a unique army — appropriate for a unique people.

In yesteryear, those who were afraid had the ability to run away from battle. Today, we cannot run away. Yet, there is an answer for us as we prepare to fight our own battles in Elul and on Rosh Hashanah.

Our armaments of choice are *teshuvah*, *tefillah*, and *tzedakah*. Our families and our communities need us to stand up and fight. It is the battle of our lives — and the battle of life itself.

KI SEITZEI
TEMPORAL VERSUS ETERNAL

S ometimes, the order of the *mitzvos* is the key to understanding their meaning. Take, for example, the first three paragraphs of *Parshas Ki Seitzei*, which begin with the mitzvah of *yifas to'ar*.[350]

If a Jewish soldier goes to war and he is attracted to a non-Jewish woman, the Torah does not immediately say, "Don't! You can't take her." In his particular circumstance of being on the battlefield, the Torah understands that if you tell him, "No," he will transgress anyway. Therefore, the Torah works with the soldier and helps him get the idea out of his system by instructing him to wait a month, etc. During this time, the physical attraction is going to wane. He will hopefully come to his senses and he will realize that this is not exactly the ideal wife for him.

However, should he take her after she has converted, the Torah permits it. The next paragraph comes and speaks of the man who has two wives. While on the Torah level, a man is permitted to have more than one wife, the Torah says that the one he loves less will really be *"snuah,"*[351] hated to him.

350 *Devarim* 21:10-14.
351 Ibid., 21:15.

What will be the end result of this situation? There are going to be children from these wives. The third paragraph, of the *ben sorer u'moreh*, literally the stubborn and rebellious son, then comes in. The Rabbis explain the link between these paragraphs: Unfortunately, one wrongdoing leading to another.

What is true in the negative is also true in the positive.

Later in the *parsha*, Rashi quotes the concept of *mitzvah goreres mitzvah*,[352] that one mitzvah leads and brings to another. We find this with regard to the mitzvah of *shiluach hakan*.[353] The Torah says, "Don't take advantage of the mother bird, which is hovering over its young in the nest." Rather, "*Shalei'ach teshalach es ha-eim*," send the mother bird away. And "*Ve'es ha-banim tikach lach*," you shall take the children for yourself.

After the Torah concludes its discussion of this mitzvah, it tells us that when you build a new home or acquire a new home you are to make a *ma'akeh*, a fence, for your roof. The Torah gives a reason for this act: "*Ve'lo sasim damim be'veisecha ki yipol ha-nofel mimenu*,"[354] so that there will be no blood caused unnecessarily in your home, lest someone fall from the (flat) roof which is upon your house.

Immediately afterwards, the Torah says that you are not to plant your vineyard *kilayim*, with a mixture of the vine and the wheat.[355] The Torah then goes on to say, "Don't plow with the ox and the donkey together,"[356] and then proceeds to say, regarding your clothing, "You shall not wear *shaatnez*, the combination of wool and linen together."[357]

What is the flow of this seemingly eclectic hodgepodge of *mitzvos*?

Rashi explains. If you fulfilled the mitzvah of sending away the mother bird, you will then be privileged to build a new house. You will thereby have the opportunity to fulfill the commandment of

---

352 See *Pirkei Avos* 4:2.
353 See *Devarim* 22:6-7.
354 Ibid., 22:8.
355 Ibid., 22:9.
356 Ibid., 22:10.
357 Ibid., 22:11.

having a fence around your roof. You will then have the opportunity of planting a vineyard in order that you will separate the seeds. Then you will have clothing in order to be able to do the mitzvah of *shaatnez*. The point is to realize that one mitzvah brings another.

The question is: What is the purpose of this fence which is being placed around the roof? At its basic level, it protects the people on the roof that they should not fall off.

Rav Yosef Salant, in his *sefer Be'er Yosef*, inserts an additional interpretation into this Rashi and the entire meaning of these *mitzvos*. If you fulfilled the mitzvah of *shiluach hakan*, the reward is not the building of the house. The reward is the ability to fulfill the mitzvah of the *ma'akeh* (not to mention the mitzvah of *mezuzah*), and for that you need a house!

This is a whole new perspective on what a house is to be. A house is not just a place to live. It is an opportunity for the mitzvah of a *ma'akeh* (and *mezuzah*).

After all is said and done, very few things are permanent in this world. That beautiful, wonderful house does *not* last forever. The only thing which does last forever is the mitzvah you did. Once you have performed the mitzvah of making a *ma'akeh*, you have made a deposit in the bank of God's *mitzvos* and that mitzvah becomes your mitzvah forever. Once you bought a kosher *mezuzah* and affixed it to the door, that mitzvah is yours forever. The house may not stand forever. However, the *mezuzah* will stay with you forever.

Rabbi Pinchas bar Chama[358] explains that *mitzvos* escort the Jew. Wherever you go, the *mitzvos* accompany you. When you build a house, you become immediately obligated in a *ma'akeh* and a *mezuzah*. When you buy clothes, you have to check them for *shaatnez*. If you are a male and you go to take a haircut, you tell the barber to please be careful not to cut off your *payos*. If you have a field, you have an opportunity to make sure that you do not have *kilayim* (seeds of one crop mixed with seeds of another crop). You cannot, in your field, plow with the ox and the donkey

---

358 *Devarim Rabbah*, Ch. 6, Par. 2.

together. *Mitzvos* are the Torah's way of taking the physical world and infusing it with spirituality.

One does not even have to go out into the field to encounter this idea. There is a true story told about the Chofetz Chaim. When he was an older man, he did not really have an appetite. The student who was taking care of him said to the family, "*Oy*! I have a problem. I can't get him to eat." In order to get him to eat, the Chofetz Chaim's daughter gave the young man an apple and said, "Here, give it to the Rebbe." The student came back and said, "I'm sorry. The Rebbe doesn't want to eat." She then said, "Watch this." She went over to the Chofetz Chaim and said, "This is a *borei pri ha-eitz*." And guess what? He ate the apple. He did not have an appetite, but he wanted to make another *brachah*. This is the way they got the Chofetz Chaim to eat!

When Rav Shach, *zt"l*, had a feeding tube put into him, he looked troubled and disturbed. They asked him, "Rebbe, does it hurt?" He said, "It doesn't hurt physically." However, he was troubled that he had the loss of *brachos* which one does not recite with a feeding tube.

The *parsha* speaks to us in the month of Elul and says, "Take a step back and realize *ashreinu ma tov chelkeinu*, how privileged we are." Look around. There is such an opportunity at every turn to perform *mitzvos*. This gives us the immortality that each of us, consciously or subconsciously, craves.

What an incredible opportunity.

KI SAVO
BEYOND RECIPROCITY

The 611ᵗʰ mitzvah in the Torah, and the last mitzvah in *Parshas Ki Savo*, is that of *"Ve'halachta be'drachav."*[359] The *Chinuch* explains the mitzvah as, *"laleches u'le'hidamos be'darchei Hashem Yisborach,"* to walk in and to emulate the ways of God.

The Rambam in *Hilchos Dayos*[360] speaks in terms of the Golden Mean, meaning not to be an extremist in terms of our character and personality development. Rather, literally, one is to proceed *be'derech ha-yashar*, in the straight path. He explains that we are commanded to conduct ourselves and live this kind of a lifestyle. The Rambam then cites from none other than *Parshas Ki Savo*, *"Ve'halachta be'drachav,"* and you shall walk in God's ways. He then quotes the commentaries[361] on this verse who explain that just as God is compassionate, so too you shall be compassionate. Just as God is merciful, you too are to be merciful. Just as God is holy, you too are to emulate God and conduct yourself in a holy manner.

---

359 *Devarim* 28:9.
360 Ch. 1.
361 Such as the *Sifri* as well as the *gemara* in *Shabbos* 133b.

A basic question needs to be asked. The Talmud will often bring a verse to substantiate a particular idea. Sometimes, the *gemara* will then ask, "*Lamah li kra*?" Why do I need a verse from the Torah? Exclaims the *gemara*, "*Sevara hu!*" It is inherently logical, something that man can understand on his own! The *gemara* accepts the point and then explains why the verse in question is necessary in that particular context.

In our case, why do we need a verse to teach us that man is to conduct himself in a good and decent manner, i.e., that he is to be kind and merciful?

Rav Pinchas Scheinberg, *zt"l* adds a beautiful insight into the uniqueness of *chesed* which the Jew is commanded to fulfill. He explains that where basic and obvious kindness ends, it is there that it begins within the Jewish people. Consider the *gemara* in *Sotah*[362] where Rebbe Simlai taught: How important is *gemilus chasadim*, the practice of kind and good deeds? It is so important that the Torah begins and ends with kindness and good deeds. That the Torah concludes with kindness and good deeds, explains the Talmud, is portrayed by that which is written in *Parshas Vezos HaBerachah*, "*Va'yikbor oso ba'guy*,"[363] and He buried him in the valley. "*Va'yikbor*" refers to God Himself, Who buried Moshe Rabbeinu.

The real question arises concerning where the Torah begins with *gemilus chasadim*. The Talmud cites the verse "*Va'yaas Hashem Elokim le'adom u'le'ishto kosnos or va'yalbishem*,"[364] God made for Adam and his wife garments of leather and He dressed them. This is the example of kindness, says the Talmud, with which the Torah begins.

Think about it, though. Isn't kindness found earlier in the Torah? Can there be a greater kindness than when God infuses into man his soul and gives him life? Isn't placing man in Gan Eden, giving him the opportunity to serve Him, a kindness? Man could have been placed in Antarctica. Instead, he is specifically placed in the Garden of Eden! Why is the first act of kindness mentioned that He clothed man and his wife?!

---

362 14a.

363 *Devarim* 34:6.

364 *Bereishis* 3:21.

Rav Scheinberg explains that all of the kindnesses which God did for Adam and Chava prior to the leather garments were done prior to the sin of man. Offering kindness to man prior to his sinning is understandable, even perhaps expected. When God continues his acts of kindness after man's sin — that is *chesed*! This is the meaning of *ve'halachta be'drachav*. It is not simply to be a "nice guy." That is obvious and doesn't require a verse. The *parsha* is teaching something that we cannot figure out on our own. We are to recognize that the concept of extending kindness is not only to someone who is kind to me. The concept of extending kindness is even to someone who unfortunately is not kind to me.

Required reading for the time of year when we read *Parshas Ki Savo* is to read through at least the first chapter of the *sefer Tomer Devorah* by Rav Moshe Cordevero. An incredible philosopher/kabbalist, he goes through the verses in the Book of *Michah*, which we recite as part of the *Tashlich*.[365] Included in these verses are the thirteen attributes of God. The *Tomer Devorah* points out that not only does God sustain man, but He even sustains the sinner. Even at the time when the sinner is sinning, God gives man the capacity to continue. He doesn't "cut off" our life energy. God gives each individual the incredible gift of life, even when they use it against Him! What *chesed*! He shows His love, even at a time when we are not at our best. Likewise, we have to extend this kindness to others.

This is what the verse of *ve'halachta be'drachav* teaches. As we are about to go into the hospital to visit someone and fulfill the mitzvah of *bikur cholim* or we are about to go into someone's home, *lo aleinu*, who is sitting *shivah*, for the mitzvah of *nichum aveilim*, we are not only to do these acts of kindness because we are good people. In addition, we are to say to ourselves as we are about to enter, "I am about to fulfill a biblical mitzvah of emulating God in this process."

What a powerful mitzvah this is! It penetrates to the very core of our being. It reminds us that *chesed* as well is to be done as a mitzvah, not simply as a humanitarian act and an instinctive good deed.

---

365 *Michah* 7:18-20.

May our focusing on this mitzvah help us not only in our daily performance of *mitzvos*, but, please God, help prepare us for the forthcoming *Yom haDin*. If we are going to be more generous and forgiving towards others, then indeed God will act similarly to us.

NITZAVIM
MERE MENTION

Rashi asks:[366] What is the connection between *Parshas Nit-zavim*, where Moshe opens with a statement "You are all standing here today" about to enter into a covenant, with the previous *parsha*'s long conclusion of no less than ninety-eight curses?

Rashi suggests that upon hearing all the curses, the faces of Israel turned pallid. They were filled with fear and exclaimed, "Who can possibly bear these?" Upon seeing the people's reaction to the mere mention of the curses, Moshe immediately began to appease them by saying, "*Atem nitzavim hayom*,"[367] you are standing today. "Even though you have angered God much through your actions," Moshe said to them, "nevertheless, He has not destroyed you. You still exist before Him." Similarly, in each and every generation, we are to derive inspiration from the words of "*Atem nitzavim*" — the very continuity of the Jewish people.

In his *sefer Darkei Mussar*, Rav Yaakov Neiman, *zt"l*, quotes a

---

366 On *Devarim* 29:12.
367 *Devarim* 29:9.

very interesting insight in the name of Rav Leib Chasman, who was the *mashgiach ruchani* of the *Chevron Yeshiva*. Rav Chasman comments on the frightened reaction of the Jewish people upon hearing the curses. Moshe explains to them that the very threat of the punishments mentioned in the curses in and of itself caused them to get into shape. That is why they are standing here today: The fear itself caused them to repent. They did not need the actual punishments; the fear of the punishment itself was sufficient.

Rav Neiman quotes as well the Dubno Maggid, who, in his own style, always has an interesting parable to bring the point across. This may be compared, he says, to a young man from a very wealthy family who was once sick. Needless to say, this man was accustomed to only the finest food prepared in the most sanitary conditions and eaten in a most luxurious fashion. The doctors determined that it was necessary for this young man to vomit in order to help him in his recovery process, and decided to prepare a bitter potion for him to drink which would cause him to vomit. The doctor was very clever. He started to prepare the potion near the sick young man. The mere sight and smell of the potion was enough to make the sensitivite young man vomit. He didn't need to actually drink it.

Similarly, the Jewish people did not have to drink from the curses of *tochachah* in order to recover from their spiritual illness. Rather, the very hearing of these curses was sufficient to help them get back on track. What a powerful lesson this is!

The *gemara* in *Megillah*[368] relates that Ezra haSofer ordained that we read the curses in *Parshas Ki Savo* annually prior to Rosh Hashanah. Tosfos explains how *Parshas Nitzavim* is the buffer between the curses and the *Yom haDin*, Judgment Day, of Rosh Hashanah. Why? "*She'tichle ha-shanah ve'kililoseha,*" so that the year may end with its curses.

What does it mean that our reading the curses "ends the year" with its curses?

Perhaps we can suggest the following, based upon the *Or*

---

368 31b.

Yahel.[369] The Torah tells us in the sixth chapter of *Sefer Vayikra*, "*Zos toras hachatas*,"[370] this is the law of the *korban chatas*. The *gemara* in *Menachos*[371] teaches[372] that since we do not have a Beis Hamikdash today and cannot perform the *Avodah*, our studying the *chatas* is the equivalent of bringing it.

Similarly, suggests Rav Chasman, you are to listen to the curses and take them seriously. The simple hearing of the curses is to inspire within you the realization that there is a God. In addition, you are to recognize that *yesh din ve'yesh dayan*, there is a judge and there is a plan to the world. There is also accountability, which makes us responsible for everything that we do. If listening to the curses being read in *shul* serves its intended purpose of bringing you to this realization, then this process will, on its own, be sufficient. In other words, we will not have to experience the physical manifestation of the curses as long as we listen well to their warnings.

When we, however, let these readings simply roll off our backs and ignore them, then we are in trouble. If we do not take the threat seriously, the next step is the actual implementation of the threats, God forbid.

The Torah says in many places that if someone commits a particularly serious *aveirah*, such as violating Shabbos or worshipping *avodah zarah*, they are *chayav misah*, they get the death penalty. How many times was someone actually put to death for violating such a mitzvah? It hardly ever happened. Why? It is due to the technicalities of the law. For example, the witnesses had to warn the person immediately prior to his committing such a sin and the person had to explicitly state, "I'm going to do it anyway." The likelihood of this happening, and the fact that the witnesses had to know exactly what they were warning the person about, made this kind of a punishment very infrequent. The Talmud[373] relates that if the court would

---

369 Rav Yehuda Leib Chasman.
370 *Vayikra* 6:18.
371 110a.
372 In the name of Rabbi Yitzchak.
373 *Makkos* 7a.

decree the death penalty once in seven years, and others say once in seventy years, it was a bloodthirsty court. The verses speak of the death penalty often, though, because *we* need to know that Shabbos can yield *skilah* (stoning). This is what keeps us on our toes. We are thereby quite careful not to break Shabbos because of what it *could* come to.

Similarly, let us take the *klalos* (curses) to heart. Let us, please God, pray that by realizing what *could* happen, it should be our fulfillment thereof. May it truly be for all of us *tichleh shanah ve'kililoseha* — may the year with all its unfortunate circumstances come to a close, and may it be for all of us *tachel shanah u'birchoseha*, may the new year, please God, arrive with all its blessings.

VAYELECH
CHILDLIKE

The 612th mitzvah, in our *parsha*, is a mitzvah which happens once in seven years. In the year following the *shmittah* year, on the holiday of Sukkos, the Torah tells us, "*Hakhel es ha-am ha-anashim ve'ha-nashim ve'ha-taf*,"[374] gather the entire nation, the men, the women and the small children. This massive gathering of the people is for the purpose of coming to the Beis Hamikdash, where the king of Israel reads the Torah to the entire assembly.

The *gemara* in the beginning of *Chagiga*[375] asks a very basic question. It is understandable that the men are coming to learn the Torah. The women are coming *lishmoa*, to listen, so that they will have a deeper and better appreciation of the performance of *mitzvos*. However, why are the young children being brought to the Beis Hamikdash? The *gemara* answers that the young children are being brought to provide a reward for those who bring them.

This statement can be understood on several levels. The simplest

---

374 *Devarim* 31:12.
375 *Chagiga* 3a.

level is that since all the adults have to attend, they will be bringing the young children anyway. The Torah thus is giving you a bonus by making it a mitzvah, and giving you reward for what you would have had to do anyway.

A deeper understanding is that there is a reward because it is going to make an impression upon them. As Tosfos[376] comments, this is the source for the practice to bring young children to the synagogue. As soon as the children can behave in the synagogue (but not before!), there is great value in bringing them. Even though they do not understand what is going on around them, their beautiful, precious souls absorb the spirituality.

One of my colleagues once made the following point. What is this reward that the parents receive? Renewed enthusiasm. Even something as precious as the Beis Hamikdash could become boring. "I've been there. I've done it time and time again," a person may say. However, when one sees the excitement expressed by the child when he sees the Beis Hamikdash, this gives the parents an opportunity of re-evaluating that which they take for granted.

Compare two adults who go together to the zoo. One goes with another adult. One goes with a child. See what kind of a different experience it is seeing it through the child's eyes.

The Torah is teaching us that from time to time, it is important to be able to look at things through the eyes of a child and to look at life from a different perspective.

We begin the recitation of *Selichos*, in most years, on the *Motzai Shabbos* immediately prior to Rosh Hashanah. *Selichos*, as a term, means forgiveness and pardon. In a human court, one cannot simply make a court appearance. Rather, one has to hire a lawyer, he has to understand the charges against him, how he is going to plead, etc. It all needs to be well-thought out before he arrives in court and appears before the judge. This is exactly what we are doing with the recitation of *Selichos*.

Many of us find *Selichos* difficult to relate to. So much can be learned from the very opening line of *Selichos*. The prophet Daniel

---

376 Ibid.

teaches us, *"Lecha Hashem ha-tzedakah ve'lanu boshes ha-panim,"*[377] You, God, are righteous and consistently extend goodness to all and we unfortunately are embarrassed and ashamed.

Shame is a healthy emotion for one to feel. It is hard to affect any kind of a change without it. Once again, let us look at the innocence of a child. A child, between the ages of approximately three and six when he is caught doing something wrong, feels a sense of shame. The child does not look for excuses.

At *Selichos*, each and every person must look into himself and identify at least that one area in which *"lanu boshes ha-panim,"* in which we unfortunately have that egg on our face, i.e., that bit of embarrassment. This is a healthy kind of emotion. This is, after all, going to be the first step, which will precipitate some real change within the person's behavior.

If one does not feel some element of shame when they pick up the *Selichos* book, they are wasting their time. *Selichos* is not a mere recitation. While reciting *Selichos*, you should be speaking to yourself and you should understand that you have not been perfect in all areas and there is definitely room for improvement. Unless you can identify that area of shame within yourself, *Selichos* is not going to be meaningful.

Let us close with a verse where Yehuda is speaking, not knowing he is speaking to his brother Yosef. He says in his passionate plea, *"Eich e'eleh el avi ve'ha-na'ar einenu iti"*[378] — How can I go up to my father (Yaakov), and the young lad (Binyamin), is not with me? Many of the Chassidic masters, Rav Meir of Parmishlan, the Chidushei Ha'Rim and others see a second layer of meaning in this question: How can I go up to my Father in heaven when the youthfulness is not with me?

We have to learn from young children — their innocence, their sense of shame and their excitement at experiencing new things. Please God, we should be able en masse to incorporate this youthfulness into our lives as we anxiously gather in synagogues across the world and begin to prepare for our court appearance in front of the King of kings.

---

377 *Daniel* 9:7.
378 *Bereishis* 44:34.

HA'AZINU
SWEETNESS OF TORAH

arshas Ha'azinu is an exceptional *parsha* in that the great majority of the *parsha* is poetry. There is something remarkably different between poetry and prose. Prose is understood merely on the surface of the text. In regard to poetry, on the other hand, the more you know about the author, the more you can appreciate the nuances, because poetry and its author are closely intertwined. The author of this poem is none other than God Himself. Therefore, the more we study the *shirah* of *Ha'azinu*, the more we discover about God and the more we are able to understand the very special relationship we have with Him.

The *gemara* in *Rosh Hashanah*[379] tells us that the *shirah* of *Ha'azinu* can be divided into six parts. One section per week was read in the Beis Hamikdash on Shabbos afternoon. In other words, each Shabbos they read one-sixth of the *shirah* of *Ha'azinu*.

The Seforno fleshes out the structure of its six sections. First, there is an introduction. The second part explains how God manipulates history to develop for the benefit of man, and then chooses Israel.

---

379 31a.

The third part tells the specific history of the Jewish people. Hashem granted the Jewish people happiness but unfortunately they repaid Him with bad instead of good. This is why they deserve the severe punishment — the subject of the next section.

The fourth part of the *shirah* describes the fall of Israel from the greatest heights to the lowest depths, to the extent that they were worthy of being, God forbid, utterly destroyed.

The fifth part gives the reason for why the Jewish people were not destroyed — it would have been a *chilul Hashem*. The nations of the world would have said, "See, He could not maintain His people."

This is an incredible idea. The very identity of the Jewish people is inextricably bound to that of God Himself. The destiny and the eternity of the Jewish people is guaranteed by this *shirah*.

Finally, the sixth and final part of this *shirah* describes our redemption, and the ultimate revenge against those who have harmed us.

The Ramban[380] writes that had this *shirah* been written by non-Jewish astrologers, it would have been worthy of belief, because everything contained within has been fulfilled to this day. Nothing has been in error. He writes, how much more so do we believe in and trust completely the words of God by His prophet who was the most faithful in His house!

According to the *Sefer haChinuch*, who follows the Rambam, there are no *mitzvos* in this *parsha*. According to the Ramban, however, the last of the 613 *mitzvos* appears here — the mitzvah of *birkas haTorah*.

The Ramban learns that, aside from the mitzvah of studying Torah, there is a separate, independent mitzvah of *birkas haTorah*. Almost all the blessings we say are Rabbinic. The only exception to this rule, where we have a blessing in conjunction with the performance of a Torah mitzvah, is *birkas haTorah*. Before we study Torah, we recite *birkas haTorah*.

In addition, the nature of this blessing is one where the Jew says Thank you to Hakadosh Baruch Hu for giving us His Torah. We are

---

380 *Ramban Devarim 32:40.*

told in the *gemara* in *Shabbos*[381] that the angels complained to God and said, "No, You cannot give the Torah to mortal man." Moshe has to wrest the Torah from the angels. The Torah is such a special and precious gift! Through it, we are connected in a very real and literal sense to Hakadosh Baruch Hu.

How many times a day do we say this blessing? Only once. In reality, we are living Torah all day. For example, the way we talk and the way we conduct ourselves in business; all this is a reflection of the *birkas haTorah* which we recite. Our entire lives are connected to Torah.

The *gemara*[382] relates a teaching of Rav Yehuda in the name of Rav. The *navi Yirmiyahu* asked, *"Mi ha-ish he-chacham ve'yaven es zos?"*[383] "Tell me," says the prophet Yirmiyahu, "who is the wise man who can explain and understand what has happened?" In other words, why was the land destroyed? At the time of the destruction of the First Temple, not only were the people exiled but the land itself was destroyed. What was the root which caused the people to go awry and to worship idolatry, cause a breakdown of morality, and bring murder within the Jewish community?

The wise men and the prophets could not answer this question. However, God Himself explains, *"She'lo berchu ba'Torah techilah,"* they didn't say the (pre)blessing on the Torah. The *Ran*[384] understands this to mean that while they studied the Torah, they related to it as just another subject. In other words, it was not sufficiently important to them. They did not realize the privilege of studying God's Torah, and thereby connecting with Him.

The Baal Shem Tov adds depth to this. There are two blessings included in the *birkas haTorah*. Even though the second blessing, *"Asher bachar banu,"* is the primary one, the word *techilah* in Hashem's response refers to the first *brachah* of *ve'ha'arev nah*, in which we ask God to please make Torah sweet. The people did not say this

---

381 88b.
382 *Nedarim* 81a.
383 *Yirmiyahu* 9:11.
384 Ibid *Nedarim* 81a.

blessing. They studied Torah, but they did not appreciate the sweetness of Torah. They did not realize the joy of Torah. If and when one realizes the joy of Torah, the blessing continues, "*Ve'niyeh anachnu ve'tze'etza'einu*," may we and our children and the children of our children and the rest of our people, all of them, become knowledgeable and perpetuate Your Torah, God.

The key to the perpetuation of Torah is for you to show your children how happy you are with the Torah and *ve'ha'arev nah*, how sweet it is. The best guarantor for the perpetuation of Torah is the person who can demonstrate the sweetness of Torah.

The Ramban understands the verse from *Parshas Ha'azinu*, "*Ki shem Hashem ekra havu godel l'Eilokeinu*,"[385] when I call out to Hashem and ascribe greatness to our God, to refer to the final mitzvah of the Torah, namely the mitzvah of *birkas haTorah*. May we take this mitzvah seriously, and rejoice in the blessing – and learn! – with great pride and joy.

---

385 *Devarim* 32:3; *Nedarim* 81a; *Yirmiyahu* 9:11; *Devarim* 32:3.

VEZOS HABERACHAH
MORE THAN A CONCLUSION
— AN INVITATION

V ezos HaBeracha has the distinction of being read and completed under a *tallis*, amidst joy and excitement every year on Simchas Torah. Most often, it is one of those *parshiyos* that we do not have sufficient time to study. And there is so much to learn from this incredible *parsha*.

"No one knows his burial place to this day."[386] While no stone marks the grave of Moshe, Hashem gives us the epitaph that would adorn his eternal resting place. "Never again has there arisen a prophet like Moshe, whom Hashem had known face to face. As evidenced by all the signs and wonders that Hashem sent him to perform in the land of Egypt, against Pharoh and his subjects and all his land. And by all the strong hand and awesome power that Moshe performed before the eyes of all Israel."[387]

I'd like to focus on the last three words of the *parsha*, the closing phrase of the Torah. Like an onion, the Torah is so multi-leveled. On the surface, as Rashi notes, the closing phrase is alluding to Moshe's breaking of the tablets, which was done in full view of the entire

386 Ibid., 34:6.
387 34:10-12.

nation. However, I believe that this closing phrase contains much more, including philosophical and sociological insight as to the uniqueness of the Jewish nation.

To begin with, the Rambam writes in *Hilchos Yesodei Hatorah*,[388] that the Jewish nation believes in Moshe and recognizes him as a true prophet, the greatest of all history, as indeed the Torah teaches,[389] "And they will also believe in you forever." We do not believe in Moshe because of the many miracles and wonders he performed, but rather the entire nation saw/watched Moshe at the revelation at Sinai ascend the mountain, and heard Hashem call him and instruct him what to communicate to the entire nation.

"*L'einei kol Yisrael*" — in front of the eyes of all of Israel — is the personification of the uniqueness of the Jewish people. No other people on the face of this earth can claim that an entire nation experienced prophecy. The "Torah that Moshe commanded us is the heritage of the congregation of Jacob,"[390] Moshe was the prophet who taught us Torah. He actually taught us only 611 *mitzvos* (amazing that the *gematria* [numerical value] of the word "Torah" is 611!) The first two of the Ten Commandments we all heard directly from Hashem — direct revelation.

Moreover, we not only *heard* the revelation, we *saw* it as well. The Torah, immediately following the enumeration of the Ten Commandments, writes,[391] "The entire people saw the sounds." Rashi cites the *Mechilta* which says that they saw the audible, which is ordinarily impossible. What is the significance of this miracle?

The *Pesikta D'Rav Kahana*[392] explains this phenomenon with the following verse. "*Kol Hashem ba'koach*,"[393] literally, the voice of Hashem comes in power. It is understood by our Rabbis to mean as well that His voice comes in accordance with the *koach*, the

---

388 8:1.
389 *Shemos* 19:9.
390 *Devarim* 33:4.
391 *Shemos* 20:15.
392 Ch. 12.
393 *Tehillim* 29:4.

potential, of each individual. In other words, each participant at Sinai saw/understood the same teachings differently, each on their own level of intelligence and understanding. The wise King Solomon in *Koheles*[394] teaches, "The wise man has his eyes in his head." This means that seeing includes perceiving and understanding. Similarly, a math teacher might point to a complicated problem on the board and ask the class if they "see it." He is not asking if they can see the board, but whether they comprehend the material. When the Torah says they "saw," it means they understood according to their individual level and way of understanding.

The *Pesikta* continues and explains this miraculous occurrence. Don't be amazed at this individualized revelation at Sinai, after all the *mohn* descended for all Israel, yet it tasted differently to all. To the infants and young children it tasted one way, to their parents another, and to their grandparents the exact same *mohn* had a different taste.

The Torah is for everyone, and each of us will understand it in our own way. Whoever we are, whatever age we are, wherever we are, "*L'eini kol Yisrael*" is an exciting mandate and a beckoning invitation to all Israel: the Torah awaits us all!

---

394 2:14.

ABOUT THE AUTHOR

Rabbi Benjamin Yudin is a legendary figure in the NY/NJ area. He became rabbi of a new, small Shabbos minyan in New Jersey in 1969, the first Orthodox community in the area. Under his leadership, Congregation Shomrei Torah (and all of Fair Lawn) has since become a large, thriving Torah community. He has also inspired thousands of students in the Mechina Program of the James Striar School of Yeshiva University, where he formerly served as dean, and continues to teach today.

Perhaps most famously, Rabbi Yudin gives a popular radio drasha to an audience of over 50,000 every week on Nachum Segal's JM In The AM show. He has contributed to many journals and publications; this is his first book. Beloved by his community, students and listeners, Rabbi Yudin is often known as "a rabbi's rabbi."

ABOUT
MOSAICA PRESS

MOSAICA PRESS

Mosaica Press is an independent publisher of Jewish books and e-books for the broad spectrum of Jews and non-Jews. Our authors include some of the most profound, interesting, and entertaining thinkers and writers in the Jewish world today. **Mosaica Press** is responding to the great demand for high-quality Jewish works dealing with issues of the day. Our aim is to uplift, explain, and inspire. Our authors, investors, partners, clients, and customers know that we do our best to operate with honesty, integrity, and good service.

For more information please visit www.MosaicaPress.com